911.8   3̶0̶1̶.̶3̶
EVA

KW-054-791

5. 5.78

THE POLITICS
OF ENERGY

THE EMERGENCE OF THE SUPERSTATE

Douglas Evans

M

© Douglas Evans 1976

All rights reserved. No part of this publication may be
reproduced or transmitted, in any form or by any means,
without permission

First published 1976 by
THE MACMILLAN PRESS LTD
London and Basingstoke
Associated companies in New York
Dublin Melbourne Johannesburg and Madras

SBN 333 17623 5

Typeset in Great Britain by
PREFACE LIMITED
and printed in Great Britain by
REDWOOD BURN LTD
Trowbridge and Esher

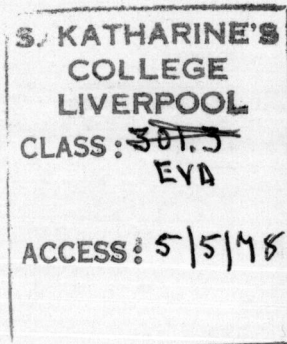

S. KATHARINE'S
COLLEGE
LIVERPOOL
CLASS: ~~301.5~~
EVA

ACCESS: 5|5|78

911.8

This book is sold subject
to the standard conditions
of the Net Book Agreement

Contents

Contents

Preface

This is not another book about the energy crisis. The body of
the book is taken up with a comparative study of the energy
policies of what I have termed the superstates – the United
States, the European Community, the Soviet Union, China and
Japan. Each chapter attempts to describe the development of
energy policy, including the internal political debate and its
likely course for the future, and pays particular attention to
external ramifications. While the analysis varies in its scope
between the United States where the energy debate has been an
open political struggle, the European Community where it has
tended to be a bureaucratic process gilded by a stylised political
debate, and the Soviet Union where it has been a balancing act
by the rulers of the Kremlin setting off the need for agricultural
and technological imports and the requirements of a new
consumerism with the traditional national security criteria,
there are many observable common features. It is the nature of
these common features that is one of the chief underlying
concerns of the book.

Indeed, since the pattern of increases in energy consumption
is well-nigh universal, it is not only energy policy but the
political and economic structures in the Communist, socialist
and mixed capitalist systems alike that are becoming increasingly similar. This book, while it attempts to document the
development of the energy policies of the five superstates, aims
to illustrate the extent to which these new structures may
represent a growing threat not only to the immediate social
amenity and future social fabric but also to the roots of
political freedom and individual liberty. In its most fundamental common consequence for the structures arising from
increased energy consumption in the Western World, for
instance, one can detect a trend towards centralisation in the
manner of the centrally controlled economies. Where the
private sector in three of the superstates has hitherto acted to a
greater or lesser degree as a check on the powers of the central

government, in the wake of an accelerated energy consumption rate it has more and more merged with the public sector. This is due less to any great ideological commitment to corporatism than to the enormous scale of financial investment necessary for energy expansion and the necessity for cast-iron political commitments in order to fulfil such long-term development programmes.

The fact that much of the motivation for increased self-sufficiency in energy by each of the superstates is supplied by national security only serves to lessen the possibility of a future dispersal of government power, since the whole defence—industrial establishment is by definition linked in each superstate to central government and only loosely accountable to effective democratic checks among the Western superstates. For implicit in the discussion of energy policy and the political structures it creates in its wake is that economic freedom is one of the most essential prerequisites for political freedom: that the ideas of Adam Smith about *laissez-faire* and free trade are complementary to those of John Stuart Mill on individual liberty. Some of these principles will be sketched in the Introduction, but the body of the book describes the political structures already evolving which can probably only be modified in the short term, however desirable it might be to reverse them altogether. As another cardinal principle the author regards the maximisation of freedom as the true goal of society and the individual as the ultimate entity in society which the state exists to serve.

This is in no way meant to preclude a high view of the state. Its importance as a repository of the consensus views of the individuals who constitute the nation is entirely compatible with individual liberty wherever the political structures which arise remain sufficiently flexible and responsive to the needs of the mass of its citizens. But with the growth in energy consumption and the consolidation of the links between the major industrial as well as energy corporations and the governments of the superstates, the trend to centralisation gathers force and, with it, less and less flexible and more and more unresponsive institutions. The indictment applies equally to Communist and to non-Communist superstates, for what the former achieved by elevating the role of the state far above the individual and concentrating their efforts on energy-intensive heavy industry to achieve economic and industrial parity with the West, the latter have achieved by placing the goals of growth and therefore of size on the highest economic pedestal and then reinforcing them by central government intervention in the name of national security or some other overriding national imperative that the majority of citizens cannot effectively resist. Thus are the modern superstate leviathans created out of a virtual energy-consuming binge whose end is nowhere in sight so far. The switch from primary energy sources to nuclear fuels in many industrialised countries only magnifies the dangers and underlines the strategic dimension to any discussion of the international politics of energy.

This brings us to another assumption that permeates the evidence and arguments of this book, namely the necessity for a form of *realpolitik* to be applied to energy questions in the international sphere. It does not help the cause of promoting more humane political and social structures to merely inveigh against excessive consumption of energy and raw materials and to propose changes so drastic that they can immediately be dismissed by men of power in both government and business. This book sets out to be radical only in the sense that it seeks to discover both first causes and ultimate effects across the whole spectrum of energy policy among the five superstates. It is not primarily concerned with solutions for some of the more obvious symptoms of the international energy problem; hence it leaves to others the analysis of the detailed consequences of the realignment that has taken place between the Arab oil states and the industrialised countries since the Yom Kippur war. Its concern is rather with the total trends in energy consumption, and how those trends can be harnessed to serve our survival and avoid our destruction by structures that have grown beyond our control.

Acknowledgements

Among those institutions whose help has proved invaluable in assembling some of the material on which this study is based are the U.S. Congressional Record, the U.S. Library of Congress, the reports of various U.S. Congressional Committees, the U.S. Information Services, the Soviet Embassy, the Sino-British Trade Council, the Anglo-Japanese Economic Institute, the Japanese Embassy and Information Services, and the European Community Information Services. For help on some of the more general aspects of the subject I am also indebted to the Organisation for Economic Cooperation and Development, Paris, the Bank for International Settlements, Zurich, and the United Nations Organisation in various parts of the world. Finally, I would like to thank the staff of the Trade Policy Research Centre, London, who have always offered me their unstinted advice and assistance on this book, as on its predecessor and companion volume *The Politics of Trade* (Macmillan, 1974), but are in no way responsible for the views expressed which are entirely personal.

In addition I am, not for the first time, greatly indebted to several individuals, notably my agent, Andrew Best of Curtis Brown Ltd, and my editor at Macmillan, T. M. Farmiloe who have both exercised great patience and tact in encouraging me to complete this modest treatise. I am also grateful to Angela Dyer and all those in the production department of The Macmillan Press who together with the printers have translated my typescript into a book.

Introduction: The Emergence of the Superstate

> This conjunction of an immense military establishment and a large arms industry is new in American experience. The total influence – economic, political, even spiritual – is felt in every city, every state house, every office of the federal government. We recognise the imperative need for this development. Yet we must not fail to comprehend its grave implications. Our toil, resources and livelihood are all involved: so is the very structure of our society.   (Dwight D. Eisenhower, 17 January 1961)

The truth of this warning made by the retiring U.S. President and former wartime commander has been fully vindicated by events in the last decade and a half. The same warning made about the military–industrial complex might be made with equal force about the structures, political as well as economic, that accompany the accelerating consumption of energy, not only in the United States but in each of the five superstates. The military–industrial complex is itself closely allied to the maintenance of a high energy consumption infrastructure. This particular energy infrastructure has arisen from the fact that for the last twenty-five years the industrialised world has become accustomed to the availability of abundant and cheap oil which in turn provided the means for an unprecedented industrial expansion. This has proceeded to such an extent that the importance of energy in determining a nation's economic and political strength is now widely accepted. Thus it is no accident that the United States and the Soviet Union are the world's main producers and consumers of energy resources. The superstate category, however, embraces not only the superpowers but also three other major concentrations of political and economic power which share certain common characteristics. Not least of these common features is a high and increasing rate of energy consumption which, if the present increase is maintained, will mean that in the last three decades of the twentieth century more energy will be required than the total amount of energy consumed prior to 1970. However, a number of other important features common to mid-twentieth-century industrialism may usefully be delineated which coincidentally achieve their apotheosis in the superstate.

One of the best compressed summaries of modern industrialism and the factors which, in combination, are typically elements in modern economic growth was provided by Sir John Hicks in his Stevenson Memorial Lecture to the Royal Institute of International Affairs, London, in November 1973. Sir John's summary was itself a précis of the arguments of another Nobel prizewinner, Professor S. Kuznetz.[1] Kuznetz, according to the Hicks précis, defined modern growth by six characteristics: (1) rapid increase in production and in population; (2) rapid increase in productivity — output in relation to input; (3) structural change, as exemplified by movement of population away from agriculture; (4) social change — urbanisation and secularisation; (5) revolution in transport and communication, making the world 'one world' as it was not before; (6) unequal growth between countries, so that some are 'advanced' while others are left behind.

These six characteristics, while they have a recognisable authenticity about them, lack a driving motive force or unifying principle which would pull together such pervasive demographic and material changes. To Kuznetz the seventh and indispensable unifying factor is 'the emergence of modern science as the basis of an advanced technology'. This is a crucial observation, and if Kuznetz is correct in identifying science-based technology as the indispensable unifying factor behind the pace of modern industrialism, it has enormous significance for both the pattern of worldwide energy consumption and the political and economic structures with which it is compatible. For such science-based technology manifestly creates increasingly high energy consumption structures, yet right up until the 1930s science-based technology was not generally accepted as an indispensable factor in industrial growth. It can reasonably be deduced that really high energy consumption is a very recent if universal aspect of industrialism. By contrast, liberal democracy, as it has developed in its various forms in the industrialised regions of Western Europe, North America and Oceania, has a much more extended parentage. There is much evidence to suggest that liberal democracy can operate effectively within an industrial society; whether it can permanently survive and prosper within the framework of a high energy consumption society is something which remains to be answered. It is not altogether absurd, for instance, to suggest that one of the primary reasons for the apparently more humane face of the Chinese as distinct from the Soviet system is the low energy consumption of the Chinese and its accompanying interaction with the political and social structures. Meanwhile the foregoing Kuznetz features of industrialism, common to Communist and non-Communist societies alike in the mid-twentieth century, bring us to examine some of the most fundamental pre-suppositions of the postwar phase of industrialism — the phase when science-based technology has raised our total world energy consumption to unforeseen levels for which the political and social long-term consequences are as yet uncalculated.

Inseparability of Economic and Political Freedom

During the last thirty years the record of economic growth in the industrialised countries in both the Communist and the non-Communist blocs shows a phenomenal expansion in their gross national products. Despite enormous disparities in the levels of material welfare and the degree of personal liberty possible under the Communist system, there has grown up a very powerful myth in the free world that economics and politics are somehow separate and very largely unconnected. Moreover, as part of this myth, there has arisen a widespread belief that individual freedom is a political problem, somehow entirely separate from material welfare which is no more than an economic problem that can readily be solved given the application of the appropriate technology. Furthermore, the belief runs, virtually any kind of political arrangement can be combined with any kind of economic arrangement.

It is the writer's view that these are all fictions, though no less powerful because they are untrue. To illustrate: it has become a widespread feature of the postwar period in Western Europe that a form of 'democratic socialism' as distinct from 'totalitarian socialism' in, say, the Russian manner was entirely feasible. As long as the mixed capitalist system prospered there were few people who were prepared to challenge the philosophical assumptions of democratic socialism. In the latter half of the 1970s the swing toward a corporatist structure where private industry operated under an economic environment closely regulated by government had become widespread in Western Europe. For the first time the principles of democratic socialism were being put to the test of whether they could in practice create material prosperity without seriously eroding individual freedom. Britain, with the invaluable legacy of a long democratic tradition, and the less valuable legacy of a very early industrial revolution, by the mid-1970s had allowed around 60 per cent of its economy to fall into the public sector, thereby providing an interesting test case for democratic socialism.

Meanwhile Western Europe as a whole provided increasing evidence, especially by the EEC central authorities as well as its member governments, of state intervention in the name of coordinating energy policy. Such intervention, if embarked upon as wholeheartedly as the EEC Commission wishes, lends support to the expectation of some that it will become more and more like its Russian counterpart in its political as well as its economic aspects, elevating the role of the bureaucrat and denigrating that of the politician as the latter becomes impotent to effect the all-important strategic decisions on energy. Under such circumstances it is not too fanciful to foresee that effective parliamentary democracy is likely to prove shortlived. At the very least it is a reasonable counter-thesis to the more optimistic expectation of those who seek the further socialisation of democratic socialism and see no dangers in a continued expansion of energy consumption. It is probably no exaggeration to say that the central concern of this volume is to suggest the probability that liberal democracy is not permanently compatible with the levels of centralisation, energy consumption and military concentrations now developing; and more than this, to suggest that such high concentrations of political and economic power as the emerging superstates are inclined to aggregate to themselves, lacking sufficient democratic checks, may reach that degree of untrammelled power which leads to delusions of omnipotence and eventually to military conflict.

Such fears are easily dismissed by some who rightly point out that the superpowers, with their enormous concentrations of political and economic power combined with unrivalled military capability, have in the postwar period confined their direct conflict to limited, localised wars, whether in Korea, Indochina or Angola. The answer to this observation is essentially twofold: first, the existence of five superstates rather than two superpowers arguably increases the chances of conflict; secondly, the most likely genesis for conflict would probably come from within the boundaries of the superstates whose citizens perceive that the liberty of the individual is threatened by an ever more centralised system, and that the contest for our future liberties is being decided in the political and economic structures now being laid.

There is a need at this point to make some positive affirmations about the nature of a free society if we are to appreciate precisely why excessive energy consumption and the political and economic structures which accompany it constitute such a potential danger. According to Professor Milton Friedman, economic arrangements play a dual role in the promotion of a free society. First, economic freedom is an end in itself in that it is integral to the wider concept. Second, economic freedom is an indispensable means toward the achievement of political freedom.

First, economic freedom as an aspect of political freedom is widely underestimated; economic arrangements, however, are important primarily because they help determine the dispersion or concentration of power. The crucial contribution of competitive capitalism is that it *separates* economic from political power, offsetting one against the other. The converse is also true so that when these economic and political forces are able to combine, the freedom of the individual immediately declines, whatever the theoretical rights of citizenship or common ownership may suggest. The inescapable and, to some, surprising evidence of history is that political freedom, at those rare moments when it has flourished, grew out of a free market system in some shape or form.

Since freedom is such a rare commodity, and the political state of most of mankind has for the most part been one of economic servitude and varying degrees of political tyranny, those periods of relative political freedom (it can never be an absolute commodity except in the minds of a Utopian idealist) are the more readily spotted. The nineteenth century and early twentieth century, when not only free trade but liberal democracy spread around the world, were historically speaking highly exceptional. The fact that they were so close to our own time has tended to give us a false sense of optimism with regard to the task of creating and maintaining freedom, not least because the changes wrought since 1914, for instance in the spheres of demography and technology, have been without parallel in history. Despite its sometimes callous attitude to the working classes at home and its subject peoples abroad, there cannot be much doubt that political freedom was closely allied with the free market and capitalist institutions in the heyday of the Victorian British Empire. Its lack of a developed social conscience towards the less privileged elements in society, while not to be dismissed or 'extenuated away', was paralleled by almost every other contemporary society.

The same debt to free market institutions can be said to be owed by the ancient Greeks in their development of democracy, equally so in the early days of the Roman Republic. That both later classical civilisations were built on slave labour systems can be neither denied nor excused; equally undeniable was that both these free exchange economies provided the platform for one of the golden periods in not only European but world civilisation. Only when the contemporary Western industrial nations have abolished migrant labour, and ended all vestiges of economic imperialism towards the developing countries, can we afford to dismiss the achievements of the classical period in European history as mere slave states, as some have done. The creation of a degree of freedom for a significant minority of the population was a signal achievement for the times and owed not a little to their free market institutions.

In case we should overstate the case for a free market system it should be made clear that a *necessary* condition for freedom is not a *sufficient* condition, as the relatively recent history of Fascist Italy and Spain, of Germany, of Japan before the First and Second World Wars, makes clear, for in each of them private enterprise was preeminent within the economic and social systems. The degree of absoluteness with which a modern totalitarian system can be imposed in twentieth-century conditions was never better illustrated than in the inglorious days of the Third Reich. The totalitarianism of the Soviet Union under Stalin was hardly less tyrannical in its cynical manipulation of the political and economic structures; the severity of its oppression of minorities in the 1930s in particular has very few parallels in modern times. It is indeed possible that conditions under even the less liberally minded Tsars provided greater personal freedom than existed in Stalinist Russia, since under the admittedly crude form of capitalism that prevailed under the later Tsars it was possible to change jobs voluntarily and informally, while the existence of private property provided an effective check to the centralised power of the state. Both of the monstrous totalitarian systems of Nazi Germany and Soviet Russia in the mid-twentieth century had it in common that they were first and foremost war economies with the necessity for centralisation that that implies; they were also the first European nations to give the very highest priority to the creation of high energy consumption heavy industry. The fact that they espoused ideologies of the extreme right and of the extreme left respectively was quite immaterial to their internal victims and opponents abroad alike.

Nothing better illustrates the interrelatedness of political and economic freedom than the fact that while the nineteenth-century Benthamites — the so-called philosophical radicals — argued the case for political freedom as a means to economic freedom (in which cause they were highly successful), their philosophical inheritors today are more inclined to argue the case for economic freedom as a means to political freedom. The switch in emphasis is more apparent than real, and represents the same response to comparable issues where the actual conditions have drastically altered. At its most basic level, against a background of universal adult suffrage and of increasing equality between the sexes, the crucial ingredient in individual freedom is the freedom to make choices in the economic sphere, not once or twice but constantly. With the impetus of two World Wars, government intervention had been greatly accelerated in Europe and North America, and with it a switch in emphasis from freedom to welfare as the hallmark of a humane democracy. A minority of twentieth-century thinkers recognised early the threat to individual liberty in any trend which incorporated a steady movement toward greater and greater economic centralisation. The voices of Dicey, Hayek, Simons and now Friedman have been lifted against a trend which the evidence of this book suggests has been greatly reinforced by an uncritical increase in high energy consumption structures. The Communist superstates depict the capitalist superstates as insatiable in their appetite for energy, a true enough observation. But in their turn the Communist super-states are locked into an escalating energy consumption process, China so far less noticeably gluttonous in this respect.

It would be inaccurate to depict the trend as an unmitigated slide into political and economic centralism in one form or another. A factor, far from negligible in the 1970s, working towards freedom in both Communist and non-Communist countries is the repeated failure of central planning. Nothing has illustrated this more dramatically than the continuing débâcle in Soviet agriculture which has so consistently failed to perform up to expectations that poor climatic conditions are no longer proffered as the cause. Other trends towards greater economic freedom in the Soviet system have been the adoption of producer—consumer boards in industry and the pursuit of a markedly less autarchic foreign commercial policy.

There can never be a full appreciation of the links between political and economic freedom until the issue has been brought down to the level of the individual. Fortunately, this com-pletely accords with traditional liberal priorities. For more than any other the political liberal regards the freedom of the individual as not simply integral to any system but as the indispensable measuring rod of the efficacy or non-efficacy of any given social and political arrangements. That being the case, the liberal is committed above all else to allowing the individual to work out his own ethic. Where the traditional liberal parts company with many of his modern liberal counterparts is in his expectations of general human behaviour. Because the tradi-tional liberal saw man as basically imperfect, he saw as a natural and more or less self-evident corollary of that fact that probably the major problem of social-cum-political organisation was to provide for it by limiting bad people and enabling good people to do good, both in the abstract. In reality he knew that all people were a mixture of good and bad. The modern liberal by contrast seems to believe no such thing. He believes more or less implicitly that we are all well-intentioned and will in general behave benevolently as long as we are allowed to pursue our individual goals without too much interference by institutional authority. This can happen. In the writer's opinion it happens exceptionally and in practice does not represent the general drift of human behaviour at even the best of times. But by postwar standards of freedom and stability in the Western world these are not the best of times; they are exceptionally unstable, as the existence of 15 million unemployed and raging inflation, widespread terrorism, and so on, among the six Western industrial nations that met at Rambouillet in late 1975 testifies. Such diverging assumptions among the ranks of those who call themselves liberal democrats merely illustrate the complexity of the abstract debate.

Meanwhile, political freedom is not something that exists simply in the abstract. In many ways it can best be defined in the negative. That is, freedom is the absence of coercion of one man by another or any combination of other men. This may appear far too minimalist a definition for many people brought up on more elevated notions of what freedom is all about. Nevertheless, the fundamental threat to freedom is essentially the power to coerce. Part of the obfuscation of the political debate in modern times is to deny the presence of coercion when it exists in new and more sophisticated forms. Anyone can recognise coercion in the form of a gun if he is confronted by a gangster or political terrorist, or an army if it is arrayed in force before his country's borders, or a monopoly if he is squeezed out of business by either government, business or labour. But coercion by stealth is less easy to recognise. It is such coercion – accomplished by long-term pressures and trends, in short an accumulation of forces in a particular direction – that creates the most insidious threat to liberty because it eats into the apparently solid bulwarks of society like an army of woodworms when all the while its citizens are anticipating the crushing blows of the axe wielded by an external enemy.

To illustrate how energy policy often fits into this category with an only partly hypothetical example: the EEC Commission proposals for a common energy policy embrace a virtual two-tier system of measures, one for the next decade, the other for the next twenty-five years. If one were to assume that all of their proposals for the next twenty-five years were to be adopted by the Council of Ministers, which is clearly improbable though hypothetically possible, the immediate consequences for the general population of the Community would scarcely be noticeable. The concrete long-term consequences for the Community by contrast would be staggering. Moreover, such is the scale of the investment required, and the power and complexity of the structures necessary to channel vast resources into the political economy of the Nine, that before long the members will have attained a degree of entrenchment within the system difficult to brook. Nothing is clearer from the evidence surveyed in this book than that energy policy is characterised by achieving a certain momentum of its own once it is set on course. This is not difficult to understand when one remembers the time it takes to bring a nuclear power policy to fruition. Meanwhile the efforts of the people's elected representatives to reverse or even merely modify policies which have been evolved within some unknown recess of a bureaucratic labyrinth stretching across the increasingly hazy boundaries between the public and private sectors are likely to prove an entirely fruitless exercise — unless, that is, the juggernaut of energy policy is strictly monitored and widely debated from its inception. The point worth making is that in the most effective forms of coercion, the conflict of interest is either so unequal or so muffled that nobody knows that it is taking place until it has been virtually decided, at which point it may well suit the purposes of the victor to extend the debate to give the appearance of an open contest (referenda often fit this category).

Once it has been established that coercion may be derived from many different sources and assume a multitude of forms, be they hereditary monarchies, military dictatorships, entrenched economic oligarchies or even a momentary, fragile parliamentary majority, one can begin to apply the continual remedy of constantly paring down any disproportionate concentration of power. Coercion appears to be as much an attitude of mind as any clearly identifiable political system (though a closed system logically tends to breed a coercive attitude of mind), an attitude involving the rejection of persuasion in favour of the exercise of unequal power or effectively force of some sort. Thus it is that freedom invariably requires the elimination of high concentrations of power as one of its most primary principles. Where that power cannot be eliminated it must be dispersed by a series of checks and balances.

It follows that by removing the *organisation* of economic activity as far as possible from institutional political control (i.e. discretionary and personal control as distinct from codes of behaviour acceptable to the political community as a whole), the market is able to minimise this very contemporary source of coercive power, the combination of government, and more especially the governments of the superstates, in alliance with their respective 'indigenous' multinational companies. By forging such close links the multinational companies have, albeit often unwittingly, switched from their traditional role of acting as a check to political authority to acting more and more as a reinforcement as their political and economic fortunes become more tightly entwined as a product of political interventionism in the market. Without arguing the toss of whether the political or the economic authority holds the greater sway in such alliances — in the long term the political authority is likely to prove the more powerful in an industrialised nation, as a general rule of thumb — the proliferation of such alliances of a corporatist nature has become common.

The inevitable question arises: given that such high concentrations of economic power have been taking place, can economic power, once concentrated, be in very practical terms effectively dispersed? The answer must be an unqualified and reassuring affirmative. There appears to be no immutable law of economic behaviour which decrees that the growth of fresh centres of economic power need be at the literal expense of existing centres of economic power. Of course it can happen, but it is not empirically speaking an inevitable development. Thus the wealth-creating process in Calfornia need not exist at the expense of the earlier industrial regions of the eastern seaboard or the area skirting the Great Lakes of the midwest.

Political power, on the other hand, appears to manifest an entirely different set of behaviour patterns whose principles strangely enough seem to have been studied far less systematically in the twentieth century than have the comparable economic patterns. Putting to one side that to separate the political from the economic on this issue is an entirely arbitrary and theoretical exercise (justified in these circumstances purely for the sake of analysis), it seems to be true that political power is notoriously difficult to decentralise, a fact only now being belatedly discovered by the central governments in both Britain and France. The longer power has been exercised at the centre, the more difficult it is to devolve power to the regions while at the same time retaining selective powers for the central authority. Apart from the observable phenomena of almost any government being reluctant to surrender any of its more important powers unless virtually forced to by overwhelming circumstances, it seems to be generally true that it is more difficult to contain several equipotent small centres of political power within the framework of a single large government than it is to allow numerous centres of economic power to develop within a single large economy. The reasons are not hard to find.

In the first place, unlike the case of economic power, there seems to be in every organised society, at almost any moment in history, a fixed total of political power which can be distributed. This means that if central government takes to itself increasing powers it must *ipso facto* take those powers from somewhere else. Ever since the nineteenth-century growth of industrialism, the central governments of nation states have been transferring power and responsibility from the regional, state and local governments to the central authority. Not only has this gradual transfer of political power been going on for more than a hundred years in many Western industrial countries, but more recently, in the postwar period, the growth of international economic interdependence has created new responsibilities, and eventually powers to match, which have accrued, almost without exception, to the central national governments. The growth of high energy consumption industries since the 1930s in particular has added further impetus to this centralising trend in political power, while the demands of national security have proved convincing reinforcement for trends already taking place. This was true during both World Wars, but it is also true now when each of the five superstates is bent on some form of energy self-sufficiency, a process which we can observe accelerates political centralisation.

Having described the political process of centralisation taking place in the very broadest of terms and observed that economic power can much more readily be dispersed, it remains to be noted that a great deal of the evidence surveyed in this book suggests a disturbing shift of both political and economic power towards the central authorities of the five superstates. One cannot escape the conclusion that such trends represent a shift towards less and less democratic structures. This is what is implicit in the growth of energy consumption at the rate and on the scale described in the body of this book. It is not so much that expanding energy consumption has yet, or even is likely to throw up in the future, any significant entirely new political or social structures, but rather that it is likely to reinforce the existing structures in such a manner as to render them incompatible with representative democracy.

The likelihood of the individual citizen's recognizing the dangers before it is too late is greatly diminished by the fact that such superstate structures as are emerging have no wish to destroy the appearance of representative democracy. Indeed, they are doubly anxious to ensure its survival in the conviction that it bestows an apparent measure of legitimacy on the real as opposed to the imagined power structure. Hence the Soviet Union maintains the fiction of the Supreme Soviet wielding political power, and the European Community not only maintains the façade of a European Parliament but is anxious to confer legitimacy on its real power structure by introducing direct elections to the so-called Parliament.

It is almost as if the mere holding of elections by any body which calls itself a parliament somehow makes the whole power structure democratic. Nothing of course could be further from the truth. The essence of a democratic society is not the superimposition of representative assemblies of one kind or another, it is a process of openness in the exercise of government, a state of mind that admits the governing class to be sufficiently accessible to those whom they govern that major government policies have the prospect of being modified in response to some expression of the popular will. The increasing absence of these conditions within the boundaries of the superstates does not augur well for the present, let alone the future, when the power of the central bureaucracy is likely to be greatly strengthened by the twin demands of high energy consumption industrialism and national security factors.

One of the contributing factors to the decline in the effectiveness of democratic practices among the three Western superstates in the postwar period has been the exaggerated reliance on legislation as a remedy for political, social and economic problems, together with an underestimation of the importance of the public and private debate that should precede all legislation. The tendency of parliamentary governments, of various ideological persuasions, to see their role as one of proclaiming detailed manifestos committing them in practice to a surfeit of legislation on matters far from central to the requirements of stable yet progressive government has brought faith in the democratic process into needless disrepute. The creation of expectations beyond the possibilities of fulfilment has always been the special danger of democracy, which demands greater individual responsibility to match the greater individual freedom that it confers. Thus accompanying the growth of centralisation and bureaucracy there has been a steady decline in representative institutions themselves. The extent to which higher energy consumption and its accompanying higher material standards for the majority have sometimes occurred at the cost of personal fulfilment and a cohesive sense of community needs closer examination, and this can only be done by looking at the pattern of energy growth, its causes and consequences.

Global Patterns in Energy Consumption

So far we have described the political effects of accelerating patterns of energy consumption on the superstates and especially their institutional structures. This could suggest that there was a uniform world trend. Nothing is further from the truth. Most obviously, the patterns of energy consumption in industrialised countries differ fundamentally from those in non-industrialised societies. The non-industrialised world, which still comprises the majority of mankind, roughly 70 per cent of the total world population, is still heavily reliant on traditional energy sources that have not significantly changed for centuries. These sources include almost entirely 'local' energy made available through agencies of food, work animal feed, fuel wood, fuel dung, agricultural wastes, windpower and direct water-power. Such energy sources represent a very small *per capita* consumption, only a few times the food energy required to sustain life. Moreover, the non-industrialised world consumes only enough fossil fuels and hydro-power to double the traditional energy sources. Since almost all of its non-traditional energy is consumed by about 10 per cent of the population in the non-industrialised societies, its importance remains less pervasive than might first appear to be the case. The quite striking aspect of the traditional energy sources viewed through the eyes of energy-satiated Western industrial societies is that they are increasingly being reconsidered for reintroduction in the industrial nations. Thus natural animal waste rather than artificial fertilisers, agricultural waste rather than grain to fatten hogs, wind power, direct water power and solar storage are more and more being investigated as future sources of energy in mature industrial societies. The ultimate significance of this trend, if maintained, could be enormous as a means of bringing people back on to the land, into smaller communities and away from the uncertain employment prospects and social *anomie* that urban industrial man has created for himself.

By contrast with the non-industrialised societies, the industrialised countries consume previously undreamt-of quantities of fossil fuel and electricity, the fuel consisting of coal, oil and natural gas, and the electricity generated partly from fuel, partly from falling water (i.e. hydroelectricity). Unlike the traditional energy sources which are characterised by being derived locally (and hence requiring no great long-term planning structure, far removed from the consumer, both literally and in terms of control), the fossil fuels, and to a lesser extent electricity, are shipped vast distances from their point of origin to their points of consumption. Where *per capita* energy consumption is only a few times the food energy required in the non-industrialised world, it reaches as high as a hundred times that contained in food in the industrialised countries. In short, for the industrialised world, containing some 30 per cent of the world's population (chiefly North America, Western Europe, the Soviet bloc and Oceania), energy is at present derived almost exclusively from fossil fuels and hydropower.

The Role of Technology

Just as we noted earlier the importance of science-based technology in the history of industrialism since the 1930s, so it is observable that technology has been a major influence in the effectiveness and economics of energy utilisation. While in non-industrialised societies its influence on agriculture and food production is the more crucial because food energy is a primary energy source in such societies, its greatest influence so far has been, as one might expect, in the industrialised societies. Here it has played an indispensable role in the recovery, processing and utilisation of inanimate fuels, to an extraordinary extent determining the pattern of industrialism in Communist and non-Communist societies alike. Thus, such has been the prestige of the technologically-based industries, regarded for at least the last forty years as the pacesetters of industrialism, that their advance has proceeded almost without regard to commercial or physiological, let alone environmental or humane considerations. Increasingly closely linked with governments, the aerospace industry broadly speaking provides the most numerous concrete examples of which the latest is the Anglo-French Concorde, a supreme technological achievement but commercially unviable and an environmental and energy conservation disaster.

The consequences of this technological influence on the character of Western industrialism are seen graphically in the distribution of energy consumption in the United States, where 35 per cent goes to industrial generating processes, 25 per cent to transport services and around 20 per cent in space heating; each of these three sectors is notable for being highly technologically intensive. In the 1960s, energy consumption grew in the United States on average at about 5 per cent per annum, roughly on a par with the overall growth rate. During this period the distribution of consumption altered significantly in response to various social processes which have become universal among Western industrial nations. These included the movement of working people from farms to factories and offices, and more recently of women from home to factories and offices. In turn this has been accompanied by a growth in industrial and commercial establishments together with expanded transport facilities. Each of these expansions has led to a growth in total population. The non-farm working population, for instance, grew at twice the rate of the general population of the United States during the 1960s. Furthermore, the goods produced reveal a progressively higher energy content just as they also reveal a progressive increase in domestic energy consumption arising from increased material affluence. In Western industrial societies as a whole, the proportion of energy consumed by industrial and related transport enterprises remains at an overwhelming figure of about 75 per cent, while the proportion is even higher in the centrally controlled economies, despite the growth of consumerism in the 1970s in the Soviet Union and certain East European countries.

Projected Energy Consumption

Since the United States already consumes so much of the world's energy by itself, it illustrates some future possible trends among industrialised countries and may be reasonably used to demonstrate general principles in projected energy consumption. Historically, however, the history of energy consumption in the United States differs from that of many other industrial countries in certain important respects. The pre-industrialised United States appears never to have passed through a period of low *per capita* energy consumption since the first European settlers arrived; the industrial revolution of course had already commenced in Britain. The American colonists found an unimaginable energy resource waiting to be tapped, an entire continent completely covered with virgin forest (or so it appeared in the east). With such readily accessible fuel wood the settlers began consuming energy at a very high *per capita* rate for the period. By 1850, thanks to the indigenous forests, *per capita* energy consumption had already reached about half what it is today. This meant that between 1850 and 1970, U.S. energy consumption, by comparative world standards, grew relatively gradually. This early appetite for energy was probably highly important in providing the expectation and thus the stimulus to discover and exploit America's great natural energy resources of coal, oil and gas in the period from 1850 to 1970. The very gradualness of U.S. energy consumption growth tended to understate its enormous significance for the overall shape of society, a fact reinforced by the evidence that from 1940 to 1970 the price of all basic energy sources had been declining relative to the prices of other goods and services. The year 1973 registered the most dramatic about-turn in this trend, though the warning signals had been telegraphed by the OPEC countries at least two years earlier.

Accurate forecasting of future energy consumption has always been a hazardous task on a worldwide basis, not least because it rests so heavily on forecasting the total population growth rate, and also because it is difficult to take into account the possibility of a significant shift in the life style of the population in industrial countries. Technology, too, which as we have tried to demonstrate is such a significant factor in recent energy growth in residential consumption, may be expected to level off as man's appetite for consumer gadgetry begins to fade in technologically saturated countries such as the United States.

Just as coal replaced fuel wood between 1850 and 1910 in the United States, so since 1910 coal has rapidly been replaced by hydrocarbons, oil and gas. At the same time wind power and water power were somewhat more gradually being replaced by electricity between 1890 and 1940, while distillate fuels displaced railroad coal between 1920 and 1950. The American pattern set the pace for industrialism throughout the Western world until the entire industrialised world had by 1970 become 94 per cent dependent on fossil fuels. Although in 1970 no more than a third of 1 per cent of world energy consumption was derived from nuclear power sources, nuclear power promised to be one of the significant energy sources for the future, not least because nuclear fuels are practically inexhaustible, particularly if breeder reactors were found able to utilise the common isotopes of uranium and thorium. On the other hand the cost of nuclear power stations in terms of energy input prior to production, the time taken to bring them into production, and not least the dangers attendant on the disposal of nuclear waste were far from lending themselves to simple solutions.

If future energy consumption in the industrialised world is difficult to predict because of the many variables and rapid changes in the social climate as well as the technical field, it is the more so in the non-industrialised world. In the postwar periods, on a *per capita* percentage basis, the non-industrialised parts of the world have grown at about the same rate as the industrialised countries. Nevertheless their consumption of total energy (i.e. traditional energy sources as well as fossil fuels, etc.) grew substantially less rapidly than that of the industrialised countries. On the relative future consumption patterns of the industrialised and non-industrialised worlds there is much disputed ground. Some energy analysts appear to expect that *per capita* energy consumption in non-industrialised regions will increase quite rapidly in the foreseeable future to equal that of the industrialised regions. Others, among whom this author will cast his lot, believe that the consumption of energy in the non-industrialised countries is (on current performance) likely to be highly concentrated in cities. This would mean that around 10 per cent of the total population would attain the energy consumption levels of the industrialised countries while the remaining 90 per cent would remain at or near the consumption levels of traditional agrarian societies. Since a far higher proportion than 10 per cent would be drawn into the urban areas in the non-industrialised world over a comparable period, such demographic and energy distribution patterns represent a frightening prospect of energy and material consumption expectations greatly outstripping actual prospects.

To put it differently, and in a somewhat broader statistical context, the so-called saturation level of energy consumption in currently structured non-industrial regions would be only about 10 per cent *per capita* of that in the industrialised regions. Thus, since they are beginning from so small a base, and their energy growth rate has been so similar to date, the energy consumption of the non-industrial regions is likely to trail noticeably behind that of the industrialised world for a century or more, and as a proportion of total world consumption to remain more or less unchanged.

Meanwhile the superstates, whether fully formed or embryonic, are likely to have it in common that they will continue to dispose of the vast majority of the world's disposable energy. The following figures illustrate graphically the extent to which the five superstates (or at least four of them — China's future energy consumption might conceivably maintain its very low *per capita* rate) have mounted the escalator of increasing energy consumption. In 1950 world energy demand amounted to 2600 million metric tons of coal equivalent (mtce) which was composed of 1600 million tons of coal, 700 million mtce of oil, 260 million mtce of natural gas and 40 million mtce of hydro-power. By 1972, world energy demand had climbed to 7600 million mtce, of which 3350 million mtce was accounted for by oil. In late 1973 studies indicated that at the 1972 rate of increase, world energy consumption would have reached something of the order of 16 000 million mtce by 1985. In fact, since the rate of consumption has been rising overall, this is likely to prove a very cautious underestimate of energy consumed worldwide by 1985.

It must be clear from most of the foregoing evidence that it is well-nigh impossible to predict with any degree of accuracy the overall pattern of future world energy demand. It nevertheless remains a very necessary and useful exercise to examine the past trends and future possibilities (if not probabilities) of the energy policies of the five major economic powers, representing as they do the major consuming and producing states.

1 The United States

It is not possible to embark on a discussion of the energy debate within the United States without first examining the world role that postwar events and America's own inclinations led her to assume. Mid-twentieth-century world politics have been pre-occupied with the shifting balance of power between the United States and its allies and the Soviet Union and its satellites, not only as arguably the central political issue of the period, but also as the most pervasive underlying issue in widely differing regions. That it has been so is a striking reminder of the development of a new phenomenon in world affairs, the superpower, whose influence extends in sheer geographical extent far beyond the boundaries of any previous political imperium.

As a superpower the United States, for the last thirty years, has been the chief guarantor of the *status quo* in Latin America, Western Europe and, most notably, Asia. While the American presence and influence in Latin America can be traced to a long-standing commitment, since the days of the Monroe Doctrine, to act as the guardian of the Western hemisphere against the encroachments of the European powers, it has subsequently evolved into an omnipresent economic influence which cheerfully survives repeated changes of government by the Latin countries. In the realm of energy this underlying relationship has been of inestimable benefit to the United States in the case of Venezuela, which has been the recipient of more American oil investment than any single Middle Eastern state up until 1973. In Western Europe, the American presence grew not only from the liberating U.S. armies of the Second World War but from the permanent occupation of Eastern Europe by the Red Army and thus the political domination of half of Europe by the other superpower that had arisen from the conflict. The situation in Europe, though it has noticeably thawed, has remained fundamentally unchanged as between East and West for the last thirty years, with both sides feeling the necessity to maintain their respective military alliances in the shape of the North Atlantic Treaty Organisation and the Warsaw Pact. Yet it was in Asia that the United States was to become most deeply and actively embroiled, to her great cost in blood and treasure.

The professed aim of American policy in Asia for the last three decades, to which it has committed unparalleled military and financial resources, has been one of 'dis-imperialism'; that is, the creation of a hemisphere composed of numerous independent states progressively weaned into political and economic maturity alongside the numerous mixed capitalist states outside Asia. To create such a hemisphere, both to pre-empt mobilisation of the area under the hegemony of a single Asian power as the Japanese had done and at the same time to maintain the region open to U.S. trade and investment, it was necessary to place American military power between such a collection of mostly smallish (and if not small then militarily weak) states and the superior weight of any one of Japan, China or the Soviet Union. In pursuit of these general objectives the United States had already spent more than $34 thousand million by 1970 in economic and military assistance to Asian countries and probably as much as $20 thousand million on the Vietnam war alone. The truth is that the precise costs of the Korean and Vietnamese wars, the Japanese occupation, the maintenance of the Fleet to forestall a possible invasion of Taiwan and the whole armoury of the strategic nuclear air forces assigned to Asia will probably never be fully known. The grimmest fact of all is that in those thirty years practically every American killed in combat has fallen in Asia, which alone makes it the most costly undertaking of the postwar period in American government. This is also to leave uncalculated the terrible cost to the peoples of Korea and of Indochina.

Nevertheless it is possible to calculate the degree of success of America's Asian policy in terms of its economic benefits to the U.S. economy. Such benefits that have accrued must be judged meagre indeed. Not only does Asia account for less than 5 per cent of total American long-term investment abroad, but Asian nations account for only around 20 per cent of America's exports. Since total exports account for little more than 4 per cent of America's gross national product, and Japan represents almost 40 per cent of America's trade with Asian countries, the precise economic return on America's Asian policy must be rated as a pronounced failure. The truth is that while the United

States no doubt wished to reap economic advantages from a 'free Asia', her commitment to that continent arose out of her image of herself as a superpower, a superpower which saw itself challenged by first the Soviet Union and then China. Today there are three great powers in Asia — China, Japan and the Soviet Union — each on the ascendant, extending in their different ways their respective spheres of influence, be it diplomatic or economic.

This leaves the United States in the position of the superpower at large, not without a major role to play in Asia but undoubtedly less committed to the mainland of Asia than she has been for thirty years. The new phase in America's Asian policy requires her more and more to accept each of the three Asian great powers as potential if not yet actual equals. Like each of the Soviet Union, China and Japan, the United States must assess where her strategic and economic interests lie, but as a regional power with legitimate regional interests as a major trading country bordering the Pacific Ocean. This is not to suggest that the United States is suddenly to cast off the mantle of a superpower, to pretend that she is not one of the two opposing most powerful nations on earth, but rather that she must accept the verdict of recent history that she cannot any longer sustain such an active superpower role in Asia. There is little doubt that the public mood, as well as events, demanded such an imperial recession from Asia, a fact acknowledged by Dr Kissinger in the late 1960s, leading him to seek détente with both the Soviet Union and China in the knowledge that it was the indispensable prerequisite for a phased American withdrawal.

Most of the foregoing is widely accepted. There is nonetheless a new phase in America's Asian policy of particular relevance to the theme of both this chapter and this book as a whole, which might conceivably be adopted at some future date causing a partial revival of American over-involvement in Asia. The basis of that trend might be that America needs the strategic raw materials that Asia possesses. The irony is that the best endowed countries in this respect in Asia are the major Communist superstates, the Soviet Union and China, who can hardly be regarded as the most secure source to provide vital raw materials for an ideologically opposed superpower.

Apart from Indonesia, most of non-Communist Asia is generally speaking lacking in substantial energy resources, also

in ferrous and non-ferrous metals, coking coal, U-238 and
indeed most of what are regarded as the 'indispensables' to
feed modern heavy industry and the infastructure of a
superpower's war machine. Even acknowledged and admittedly
valuable commodities like tin, jute and new earths, produced
principally in Asia, can now be substituted by modern
technology without too much difficulty. None of this is to
suggest that the Asian hemisphere as a whole is without vast
strategic importance to the United States — merely that the raw
materials argument must not be deployed too glibly in the cause
of any serious investigation of the political framework of energy
and raw material allocation.

It will be apparent from this very brief introductory survey
of the American role on the world stage over the last thirty
years that in terms of her own predetermined foreign policy
goals the United States has already begun to accept a
diminished role, not simply in Asia but in the world as a whole.
It is not simply a matter of extending the scope of the Atlantic
Alliance between the countries of North America and Western
Europe to embrace Japan in the dialogue on such critical issues
as monetary organisation and energy supply and distribution,
but a more fundamental shift in the American public mood
towards a form of neo-isolationism. This may or may not be a
bad thing for the world community — it is too vast an issue to
be discussed in detail here — but it represents an important new
strand in the thinking of both government and people in the
United States which has an intimate effect on the overall energy
policy that the United States is likely to pursue in the coming
decade or more. Above all the neo-isolationist current of feeling
is likely to stimulate the drive to continental self-sufficiency in
energy and raw materials alike.

The Parameters of the Debate

With half the world's coal reserves (according to probably
over-generous U.S. estimates), billions of barrels of oil and oil
shale deposits, vast natural gas reserves, the largest gas reserves,
the largest installed nuclear capacity in the world, half the
world' hydro-electric plants, not to mention the largest pool of
combined scientific talent and managerial skills in the world,

the importance of the energy debate in the United States extends far beyond its borders to the entire international economic order. Moreover, since the United States is far and away the largest single consumer of world energy — consuming almost one third of all energy used worldwide — the U.S. debate and the balance which emerges between the energy and environmental interest, both heavily interwoven with issues about national security, take on a global significance. In energy, as in so much else in postwar economic development, what the United States does today much of the rest of the world will do tomorrow. For both of these major overall reasons, because the United States is both the largest consumer of world energy and potentially among the richest sources of energy of all kinds, and furthermore because the U.S. Government has declared itself committed to sharing with other nations the results of its research and development in the energy field, the centrality of the politics of the U.S. energy debate becomes clear.

At currently accelerating rates of consumption, it has been clear for some time that the United States will have exhausted its domestic supplies of petroleum by the mid-1980s. Since oil supplies 45 per cent of U.S. energy needs, and the more advanced nuclear technology then programmed would be unable to take up the slack in the interim, there has been something of an energy crisis looming for the United States since long before the 1973 Middle East war broke. At this point the necessity for the United States to import more oil from abroad was glaringly obvious. The prime source of the new oil imports, certainly for the short-term future, had to be the Middle East, where 75 per cent of the world's proven reserves lie along the shore and seabed of the Persian Gulf. The possibilities of Arab pressure against Israel through the cessation, restriction or price inflation of Arab oil supplies, together with an implicit potential threat to the entire industrialised world through the international money markets, was early foreseen as a chastening possibility.

In response to this threatened scenario, as early as late February and early March 1973, Senator M. (Scoop) Jackson, the Democratic Senator from Washington State, Chairman of the Interior Committee, and a possible contender for the Democratic Presidential nomination in 1976, renewed hearings on the energy crisis which he described prophetically as 'the most critical

problem – domestic or international facing the nation today'.
Meanwhile President Nixon, responding both to events and to
Congressional pressure, appointed a special assistant on energy
policy, commissioned a National Security Council study on the
impact of increasing reliance on imported fuels by the United
States, and sent ex-Treasury Secretary John Connally on a
world tour to discuss energy problems.

At this time, federal budgeting expenditure on energy
research and development reflected the traditionally low priority of energy questions in the federal government's
consciousness. While in early 1973 U.S. Government expenditure on energy was expected to reach $722 million in 1974
(compared with only $537 million in 1972), even the 1974
projections represented a mere 0.25 per cent of the total
estimated federal budget, or about one tenth of the space
programme's budget for the same year (running at about $5
billion annually). The general trend of Government policy was
to encourage voluntary conservation of existing fuels; to
promote better insulation in both new construction and
renovation of existing buildings; and to encourage a reduction
in the size and thus consumption of automobiles. The strategic
choices that seemed available appeared to be broadly threefold:
an increased reliance on foreign energy resources, an accelerated
development of advanced technology, or the conservation of
current resources. Within a few months the pressure of dramatic
international events had made the U.S. Government come down
heavily in favour of the second option, not least because as the
then Commerce Secretary Peter G. Petersen, put it in November
1973, 'Popeye is running out of cheap spinach'.

To appreciate the political nature of the trends which were
unleashed during the course of 1973, possibly for the next
decade, it is useful to examine in some detail the energy debate
and to pinpoint the conflicting interests and pressure groups as
well as the competing claims of the various sources of energy
within the United States.

In May 1971 the U.S. Senate authorised a two-year enquiry
and study of the nation's fuel and energy policies. By January
1973, as part of this enquiry, the Senate Interior Committee
heard some crucial evidence which was to drastically tilt the
scales of U.S. energy policy in favour of self-sufficiency. Two
top Pentagon officials, Barry J. Shillito, outgoing Assistant

Secretary of Defense, and Admiral Elmo R. Zumwalt, Chief of U.S. Naval Operations, warned on 22 January that increasing reliance on foreign fuels posed a threat to national security. They jointly proposed that a national oil reserve be established to enable the United States to withstand any cut-off in supplies of foreign crude oil. As Shillito put it, '... the mandatory establishment of reserve crude oil and products inventories' was urgently required. Admiral Zumwalt agreed that such a reserve would help the United States to achieve a reduction in oil prices 'and avoid the blackmail situation' if oil imports were cut off. Such a curtailment could result from an embargo by supplying countries on the outbreak of war, or by an attack on oil deliveries — one third of which would be brought in by sea in 1980, according to Zumwalt. Zumwalt indicated that the United States, which was currently importing about 23 per cent of its oil needs, would depend upon foreign sources, particularly the oil-rich but politically unstable Middle East nations, for more than half its requirements by 1980. In fiscal 1972, the Defense Department purchased nearly 48 per cent of its total procurement abroad, Zumwalt said.

Spurred on by the apparent threat to national security, on 15 February administration and Alaskan officials mapped a strategy to permit the construction of the controversial trans-Alaska pipeline, a plan which had to pass through Congress before oil from the North Slope of Alaska could reach the nation's homes. The plan depended heavily on the ability of the administration to reverse the decision of the Supreme Court which had previously upheld environmental objections to the pipeline's construction. As late as 9 February a federal appeals court had blocked the Secretary of the Interior from granting several oil companies a permit to begin construction of the pipeline designed to link the North Slope of Alaska with an ice-free port to the south. The Administration's plan thus included a blueprint for changing the law to permit the right of way for the proposed pipeline. Events abroad were ultimately to make the plan much more easily attainable than its instigators had ever dreamt possible.

Meanwhile, on 17 February, amid widespread criticism of the nation's energy policy, a new permanent sub-committee on energy was appointed by the Congressional Joint Committee on Atomic Energy. The sub-committee, to be chaired by Senator

Henry M. Jackson, who was also chairman of the Senate Interior Committee, planned a broad-based study of nuclear energy as it related to other energy resources. Parallel to this, President Nixon responded to the Pentagon evidence of 22 January by ordering an exhaustive National Security Council (NSC) study of the impact on U.S. foreign policy of increasing reliance on imported fuel, with Dr Henry Kissinger, John Ehrlichman and George Shultz overseeing the investigation. The study was requested to pay particular attention to (1) the existing oil import quota system, and (2) the national security implications of extensive reliance on the Soviet Union and the Middle East nations for both oil and natural gas.

It is worth noting here that a tax study group appointed in 1970 by the Council on Environmental Quality urged the United States to encourage the consumption of foreign oil rather than deplete domestic supplies. Oil import quotas were introduced by President Eisenhower in 1959 to curtail the import of cheap foreign oil, but with the extraordinary price rise in foreign oil, both actual and anticipated, the policy had lost much of its original rationale.

With oil preoccupying the minds of the nation's political strategists, the nuclear energy lobby issued an encouraging note by releasing an optimistic study of the increasing contribution of nuclear energy within the next quarter of a century. In a forecast issued on 7 March 1973, the U.S. Atomic Energy Commission predicted that nuclear power plants will have the capacity to generate 60 per cent of the nation's total electricity needs by the year 2000, compared with around 4 per cent at present. In the medium term, however – that is, by 1985 – the AEC has been forced to lower its estimates of electricity capacity. Meanwhile the AEC predicted that the first demonstration breeder reactor would become operational by 1980. By 2000, one third of all nuclear generating capacity would be supplied by liquid metal fast breeder reactors. About a month before the AEC report was published, the Federation of American Scientists, responding to the dangers of dissipating scarce scientific resources in the new search for energy, urged the White House to convert the AEC into an energy agency.

Meanwhile in Congress Senator Jackson, the chairman of the Interior Committee, proposed a ten year, $20 billion programme of energy research and development to create five government—industry corporations to develop new sources of energy. Jackson criticised the U.S. Government's over-concentration of nuclear power for future requirements. The five fields he proposed for substantial expansion were (1) coal liquefaction and (2) oil shale development, both to supplement petroleum supplies; (3) coal gasification, to supply 'synthetic' natural gas; (4) geothermal resources, to generate electricity; and (5) advanced power cycles, also to generate electricity.

On the overseas front the U.S. Government, prodded by prospects of increasing fuel shortages, signed an agreement on 31 March to import vast amounts of natural gas from Algeria. Under the $1.7 billion project, the El Paso Natural Gas Co. arranged to purchase one billion cubic feet of Algerian natural gas daily over twenty-five years beginning in April 1976. The deal, coupled with arrangements by other U.S. companies to purchase Algerian gas, brought the estimated daily purchases by the United States in 1976 to nearly 3 billion cubic feet, with Algeria the major source of imported gas for the U.S. east coast. Prices for such imported gas may be more than double that paid for interstate shipments of the fuel.

On 2 April, the trans-Alaska pipeline, representing a strenuous effort to decrease reliance on foreign sources of oil and gas, was dealt a severe blow when the Supreme Court refused to consider a lower court ban on construction of the pipeline. The nature of the battle between the sometimes conflicting interests of national security, economic development of the traditional postwar industrial variety, and the environment, was beginning to take shape and, as we shall see, by the end of 1973 had assumed an identifiable pattern. Basically the interests of national security, economic development and the environment maintained that order of priority, although significant concessions were made by each interest group to the lobbying of the others. Such an order also gave the utmost priority to national or at least continental self-sufficiency in energy. Not to be outdone by the activities of the defence and energy lobbies, the Environmental Protection Association (EPA) announced in mid-April that it would grant an additional year for industry to meet its air pollution standards. In the interim the EPA recommended far stricter standards than most of industry contended were feasible at that point.

The main pressures on Congress, however, still came from the powerful energy lobbies. About this time the chairman of the Federal Power Commission called on Congress to end federal control over the price of new supplies of natural gas on the interstate market. In response to this and other cumulative evidence of a future energy scarcity, a House energy task force recommended an additional $1 billion a year to be spent on long-term energy research. In particular it recommended a crash programme to develop synthetic gas from coal, broadly anticipating and expecting a Middle East oil cut-off before alternatives were fully developed. The extra cash for research, they recommended, should come from both public and private sources. The House task force predicted that the United States would be dependent on oil imports from the Middle East until 1985. Despite subsequently announced targets aimed at self-sufficiency by 1980, a date nearer 1985 than 1980 seemed the more realistic possibility.

On 18 April, President Nixon delivered to Congress his long-awaited message on the steps he would take to deal with the nation's growing energy shortage. Among those actions taken or proposed for immediate action by the President were (1) termination of the 14-year-old oil import quota system; (2) partial decontrolling of natural gas prices; (3) intensified offshore exploration of oil and gas resources; (4) construction of deep-water ports capable of handling giant oil tankers; and (5) a $130 million increase in funds for research and development of future energy resources.

Central to the President's proposals seemed to be that steps must be taken to increase domestic production by providing new incentives and opportunities for exploration and development of America's energy resources. The President said he would submit legislation to establish a new Department of Energy and Natural Resources. The President also established a three-man Special Committee on Energy to deal with top-level energy policy formulation. In what was a key paragraph, worth quoting verbatim, he said:

In order to avert a short-term fuel shortage and to keep fuel costs as low as possible, it will be necessary for us to increase fuel imports. At the same time, in order to relieve our long-term reliance on imports we must encourage the exploration and development of our domestic oil and the construction of refineries to process it.

(It is worth noting that by 1972 U.S. foreign petroleum imports totalled 4.7 million barrels per day, accounting for 29 per cent of total oil supply. The projections at that time were for substantial increases in imported petroleum, primarily from the Middle East. At the beginning of 1973 the United States was estimated likely to import 6 million barrels per day of crude oil and products. Assuming the trends existing then had continued, by 1985 the United States would have had to import from 50 to 60 per cent of its total oil supply. Much of this increase would have been due to the significant expected rise in *per capita* energy consumption.)

The President went on to outline his proposals in greater detail.

Deepwater Ports   At the end of 1971, one quarter of the worlds total oil-carrying capacity consisted of ships in the 175 000 deadweight ton class and over. However, there were no ports in the United States capable of handling ships of this size. Because the United States has a shallow continental shelf and no natural deepwater harbours, construction of deepwater ports would have to be offshore in international waters.

Natural Gas: Supply and Prices   'Natural gas is America's premium fuel. It is clear burning and this has the least detrimental effect on our environment.' But while the demand for natural gas had increased markedly, exploration and development had not kept abreast. Between 1966 and 1973, U.S. consumption of natural gas increased by more than a third to constitute 32 per cent of total U.S. energy consumption. Over the same period, however, proven and available reserves of gas decreased by one fifth. The gas shortage was due in part, according to the President, to the fact that the price of natural gas supplied to inter-state pipelines had been over-regulated. Consequently, demand had been artificially stimulated, while investment for exploration had been discouraged.

Alaskan Oil   The President urged prompt congressional action on legislation that would permit construction to begin on the trans-Alaskan oil pipeline. It is estimated the the Alaskan oil reserves, discovered in 1968, total at least 10 billion barrels. The President believed that the United States urgently needed the 2 million barrels a day which the North Slope of Alaska oil fields could readily supply. 'Such a supply', he said, 'would be equal to one third of our present import levels.' However, some opponents of the Alaska pipeline maintained that an alternative route, the Trans-Canada pipeline, could deliver oil to the mid-West where it was needed rather than in the West, where much of the Alaskan oil could end up being re-exported to Japan which it was presumed would be short of energy for the fore-seeable future.

Tax Incentives   To stimulate exploration and development of new drilling, the President asked Congress to extend investment tax credit provisions to the oil and gas industry by providing a 7 per cent tax credit on 'dry' or unsuccessful new wells, and a 12 per cent credit for 'wet' or successful wells.

Outer Continental Shelf   A massive effort to tap vast reserves of oil and gas from the oceans would be undertaken, with the aim of tripling, by 1979, acreage leased on the outer continental shelf for drilling oil and gas. The effort was planned to begin in the Pacific, then expanded in 1974 to the Gulf of Mexico, to include areas beyond the 200 metre isobath depth. Meanwhile the President also directed the Council on Environmental Quality to complete studies within one year on the environmental impact of drilling on the Atlantic outer continental shelf and the Gulf of Alaska. By 1985, the accelerated leasing emphasis proposed by the President could increase annual energy production by an estimated 1.5 billion barrels of oil (approximately 16 per cent of U.S. oil requirements in that year), plus 5 trillion cubic feet of natural gas (approximately 20 per cent of expected demand for natural gas). Excluded from offshore exploration was the Santa Barbara channel (California).

Coal Production and Clean Air   Although coal is America's most abundant and least costly domestic source of energy, its production has been limited by competition from natural gas, 'a competition which has been artificially induced by federal price regulation but also by emerging environmental concerns and minor health and safety requirements'.

Future Energy Sources

Shale Oil   Although recoverable deposits of shale oil in the continental shelf of the United States have been estimated at

600 billion barrels, there has been no commercial production of shale oil in the United States so far. However, a prototype shale oil leasing programme was already under way by the first half of 1973. The pilot project was planned to include the offering of six leases, under competitive bidding, of 5120 acres each, two each in Colorado, Utah and Wyoming. The six leases would support a combined production level of no more than 250 000 barrels a day. (A year after the Presidents speech it became known that a U.S. Atomic Energy Commission report claimed that this target could not be reached until 1985, thus conflicting with the Department of the Interior's target of one million barrels of oil per day by 1980.)

Geothermal Energy   A federal plan was under consideration to study the possibility of leasing federal lands for the development of geothermal energy, using the natural heat of the earth.

Nuclear Energy   There were thirty nuclear power plants already in existence in the United States in early 1973. At the same time, of all the new electricity generating capacity controlled by the Federal Government, around 70 per cent was nuclear powered. By 1980 it was predicted that the amount of electricity generated by nuclear reactors will be equivalent to 1.25 billion barrels of oil or 8 trillion cubic feet of natural gas. At the current reckoning nuclear power could provide 25 per cent of electrical production by 1980 and 50 per cent by 2000.

Clearly, if U.S. energy needs were to be met by the combined efforts of both the public and the private sectors, the effort and expenditure devoted to research and development had to be significantly stepped up.

Research and Development   The President stressed that in the short-term future a comprehensive research and development strategy had to be devised to provide the new technology to extract and utilise existing fossil fuels in a manner compatible with a healthy environment. In the longer term, that is from around 1985 to 2000, there would have to be a more sophisticated development of (1) fossil fuel resources and (2) liquid metal fast breeder reactors. In the distant future the new technologies of nuclear fusion and solar power would eventually provide a boundless supply of clean energy, but the interim period would provide the greatest challenge to the nation's resourcefulness.

On the key question of the immediate budget allocation toward research and development, the President proposed a fiscal 1974 budget of $771.8 million for federal energy research and development programmes, an increase of $129.5 million on fiscal 1973. The 1974 budget allowed for a central energy fund with the Interior Department to provide additional money for non-nuclear research and development; previously the U.S. Atomic Energy Commission had exercised a virtual monopoly over major expenditures for alternative energy sources. The new funds were mostly expected to be earmarked for coal research — especially the solvent refined coal process — and liquid metal fast breeder reactors, hopefully solving the acute problems of nuclear waste disposal and reactor safety. The U.S. Atomic Energy Commission believed at this time in the feasibility of controlled thermonuclear fusion by negative confinement 'in the near future'.

1971 Energy Message to Congress

Before summarising Nixon's April 1973 speech to Congress on the energy question it is useful to examine the main features of his earlier major message to Congress on the same subject in 1971. Among its four most important practical effects were:

(1) expanded research and development to obtain more clean energy
(2) increased availability of energy resources located on federal lands
(3) increased effort in the development of nuclear power
(4) a new Federal organisation to plan and manage energy programs.

Two years later, expenditure on energy research and development had increased by 50 per cent.

In the sense that the course America adopts on the whole energy, environment and resources question will strongly influence the direction most other industrial countries in the Western world follow, its global significance can scarcely be underestimated. To the extent that it represents the best available short summary of the ingredients of America's long-term energy problems and the most likely overall policy solutions, President Nixon's speech of 18 April 1973 is a key document. A summary of its major conclusions is therefore appropriate.

Summary of Nixon Speech of 18 April 1973

Although the United States represents only about 6 per cent of the world's total population, it currently consumes almost one third of all energy consumed annually throughout the world. Even more disturbingly, at current rates of growth in energy consumption, the United State's requirements in energy by 1985 will have doubled what they were in 1970. To match this colossal growth in demand the United States has access to three major sources of fossil fuels. It contains within its borders (1) more than 50 per cent of the world's total reserves of coal, likely to last for another 100 years or more; (2) 2000 trillion cubic feet of natural gas; and (3) potential resources of billions of barrels of recoverable oil and shale oil. At present over 90 per cent of U.S. energy comes from three sources – natural gas, coal and petroleum. Their respective advantages are, for natural gas, that it is the cleanest, but it is also the most scarce; for coal, that it is the most plentiful, but that it creates the worst environmental problems; for oil (formerly cheap and plentiful), that with domestic production no longer capable of meeting demand it will gradually become both restricted and expensive.

In terms of the policy alternatives, the following passage from President Nixon's speech sums up the conflict of interests which is likely to repeat itself in country after country and continent after continent during the next decade, first in the Western world, then in the Soviet bloc countries and thereafter throughout the world. The statement is based on the immediate threat of an energy shortage, but its application should be seen to embrace the whole range of raw materials and natural resources.

In determining how we shall expand and develop these resources, along with others such as nuclear power, we must take into account not only our economic goals, but also our environmental goals and our national security goals. Each of

these areas is profoundly affected by your decisions concerning energy. If we are to maintain the vigour of our
economy, the health of our environment, and the security of
our energy resources, it is essential that we strike the right
balance among these priorities.

President Nixon's response to these conflicting national requirements at that time can be summarised in a five-point action
programme. They included the following objectives:

(1) Increase domestic production of all forms of energy.
(2) Act to conserve energy more effectively.
(3) Strive to meet energy needs at the lowest cost consistent
with national security and the national environment.
(4) Act in concert with other nations to conduct research in
the energy fields and to find ways to prevent serious shortages.
(As a slightly ironic postscript to the aspirations towards
international cooperation in the energy field, it is worth noting
that about this time an Organisation for Economic Cooperation
and Development (OECD) report recommended the hammering
out of an agreement for sharing oil in times of acute shortages, a
proposal involving discussions between the United States, the
EEC and the Soviet Union. In the light of events in the Middle
East a few months later this proposal was somewhat sanguine
about the politics of global energy.)
(5) Apply vast scientific and technical capacity — both public and private — so that the nation might utilise its current
energy resources more wisely and develop new sources and new
forms of energy.

So much for the Nixon energy strategy at this stage. Although
Congress gave the President's proposals a generally favourable
reception, this was far from unanimous. Senator Jackson,
chairman of the Interior Committee, summed up the President's
speech and its budgetary proposals in particular as 'inadequate'.
Jackson proposed instead a ten-year, $20 billion programme of
energy research and development. He also criticised the absence
of regulations to conserve energy. By the end of June the
President had moved towards a more ambitious energy strategy
very much along the lines which Senator Jackson had recommended in mid-April. It entailed the establishment of an Energy
Policy Office to coordinate energy policies, a four-point

programme for dealing with energy problems and a $10 billion, five-year energy research and development effort, beginning in 1975. By November, as we shall see, this extension of the Presidential energy strategy was to be superseded by the even more ambitious programme known loosely as Project Independence.

In July, at a UNESCO solar energy conference in Paris attended by 800 energy experts drawn from sixty countries, the president of the International Solar Energy Society, Mr J. A. Duffie, warned that 'neither solar nor nuclear energy can be used as a "quick fix" to the energy problem. It takes ten years to put in a thermonuclear plant — thus oil imports cannot be simply and quickly eliminated.' Nevertheless, sun-powered home heating and cooling was conceivable in the near future. (Heating and cooling currently consumes 20 per cent of U.S. energy — solar energy could take care of 10 per cent fairly readily). Another prediction made at the Paris conference, this time by a building consultant to the General Services Administration (GSA), Mr Fred S. Derbins, was that solar energy 'should be more economical than electricity by the late 1970s, and in other areas cheaper than oil and gas at today's prices by the 1980s'. The conference registered a consensus view that solar-powered heating and cooling systems could be in mass use, at least in the United States, by 1980.

Meanwhile, back in Congress, the end of July saw the House Interior Committee vote for a Bill clearing the way for the trans-Alaska pipeline. Nevertheless some serious criticism of the Bill was expressed in the Committee and placed on the record. They included the view:

> By allowing control of the trans-Alaska pipeline monopoly to remain in the hands of the consortium of oil companies which already own oil rights in Alaska, the bill practically guarantees that no other oil companies will make any serious efforts to explore for additional oil reserves on the north slope of Alaska.

Others were predictably critical of the 'breaching of the National Environmental Policy Act' by the Bill. The nature of the oil companies' lobby in the United States alluded to in these criticisms of the pipeline Bill will be examined in some detail later in this chapter.

Parallel to the public and highly contentious struggle between
the oil company lobbyists and the environmentalists over the
trans-Alaska pipeline, with its obvious and immediate relevance
to the energy problem, was a much less publicised but
nonetheless highly significant swing to coordinate energy and
natural resource policies on a federal level. This took concrete
form in the shape of two Bills. The first of these was designed
to establish a Department of Energy and Natural Resources
which would take over the responsibilities of the Interior
Department, absorb the National Oceanic and Atmospheric
Administration from the Department of Commerce and generally upgrade the consideration of energy within the context of
natural resources. It would not, however, assume responsibility
for energy research and development, which would be catered
for under a separate Bill creating an Energy Research and
Development Administration. This body would in addition take
on all the existing functions of the U.S. Atomic Energy
Commission, under increasing criticism for absorbing almost all
federal energy research until very recently.

In spite of the Nixon Administration's evident awareness of
the scope of the energy problem, the mere proposal of
legislation has never been sufficient to enable the Federal
Government to chart a radically different course for a national
economy as diverse and externally pervasive as that of the
United States. There has invariably been the need for circumstances to come together in such a manner that the public can
discern that its individual short and long-term interests coincide
with the nation's. Such a conjunction began to emerge in the
fall of 1973 in a manner which made every American aware of
the energy problem as never before.

Seizing upon threats by Arab leaders to curtail oil exports,
the Nixon Administration began a new campaign to persuade
Congress and state governments to adopt its proposed remedies
for a threatening energy crisis. As from 8 September it became
possible to summarise the Government's aims on energy
publicly in a single sentence, namely to create national
self-sufficiency in energy for reasons of national security. The
President did not mention Israel at his 8 September press
briefing, but the message was clear: if supporters of Israel
wanted the United States to remain strong against pressures by
Arab nations, they would be wise to support the Adminis-

tration's energy programmes. It became apparent that, if successful, this single and fundamental appeal to the American people could serve to outflank the combined forces of the environmentalists on strip mining, the opponents of the trans-Alaska pipeline, the proponents of greater safety in nuclear energy and the advocates of improved clean air standards — at a stroke.

Against an international background which tended to reinforce the lateness of the hour, the President saw it to be a propitious moment to request Congress to pass promptly four Bills dealing with the long-range energy problems, namely the Alaskan Pipeline, Deepwater Ports, Natural Gas Prices and Strip Mining Legislation. To facilitate the enactment of the stepped-up strip mining of coal legislation the Interior Secretary, Rogers C. B. Morton, pointed out that America's ground energy reserves consisted of 4 per cent in oil, 3 per cent in natural gas and 91 per cent in coal. Clearly coal must be given a greater relative priority. Meanwhile the Secretary promised that nuclear power for peaceful purposes would be a major new initiative from then on for the balance of the Nixon Administration. The Interior Secretary made it clear that 'the United States would prefer to import oil from the Mideast, from Venezuela and from Canada — but we cannot afford to have these supplies at risk'.

While officials of the Atomic Energy Commission maintained that the safety record of U.S. nuclear plants was satisfactory, Ralph Nader predicted that public concern over reactor safety would not only grow but would actually halt reactor development within five years. By mid-1973 some 36 nuclear-powered electric plants were in operation in the United States with another 200 or so in various stages of development. The AEC blamed licensing and court challenges by the environmentalists for delays in reactor development. As at June 1973 nuclear power reactors in the United States stood as follows:

Nuclear plant capacity
in kilowatts:

operable	19 000 000
being built	51 000 000
planned	86 000 000

It was announced by the AEC in mid-1973 that a

comprehensive report on the environmental effects of the fast breeder reactor would be available in about a year.

By October the President had switched his appeal to a twofold goal of cutting energy consumption as well as attaining self-sufficiency. The outbreak of war in the Middle East threatened either a reduction or even a complete cut-off of oil. This in turn raised the spectre of rising prices and possible rationing. But not only oil shortages were on the horizon. Conservation of America's natural resources began to take the form of personal appeals to change 'our life style', legislative proposals and executive orders to protect and conserve the water, trees, land and air. Among the legislative energy proposals in the pipeline the Senate passed a Bill regulating strip mining for coal and considered legislation to save the forests, while the House Committee on Public Works warned of impending major crises in U.S. water supply and called for environmental controls on flood control projects. Indeed the Administration and Congress were now vying with each other in presenting plans for mandatory fuel allocation, natural gas price deregulation and energy conservation generally. None of this was surprising when you recall that at this point the United States imported about one third of its oil, and around 20 per cent of that from the Middle East. In the winter of 1973–4 oil imports would normally have been at the rate of 600 000 barrels per day for 150–180 days.

On 10 October President Nixon called on U.S. scientists to develop new domestic sources of energy. At the same time the President set a goal of 5 per cent in energy reduction in the private sector of energy consumption, mostly private cars and home heating. Industry, commerce and transport account for more than 70 per cent of U.S. energy consumption. Meanwhile the Democrats in Congress were critical of voluntary restraints on energy consumption and pushed hard for legislative backing for the various public appeals to conserve resources.

Coal Strip Mining: Energy vs Environment

More than 50 per cent of surface mining in the United States is for minerals other than coal; nevertheless the 1973 debate over strip mining revolved almost entirely around coal as a central energy resource. The major thrust of Congressional activity during this period has been towards a selective ban, but there is no doubt that the effects on the ground have frequently been quite devastating. According to the Environmental Protection Agency, for instance, there are 20 000 miles of high walls of waste material equalling around two thirds of the entire inter-state highway system. The worst examples are in Appalachia.

The U.S. Office of Coal Research estimates that U.S. energy consumption will double by the year 2000; moreover, between 1971 and 2000 it estimates that the United States will consume more energy than it did in all its previous history. Coal from surface mines plays a crucial role in electric power generation. Coal generated more than 50 per cent of electric power consumed in the United States in 1971, with 60 per cent of this coming from surface mines. By 1981 surface mining is likely to provide 67 per cent of all electric power. Coal production from surface mines exceeded that from underground mines for the first time in 1971. The Bureau of Mines estimates that surface mined coal costs on average $5.28 per ton, compared with $8.87 per ton for underground coal. All this suggests that the pressures behind the maintenance and even expansion of strip mining cannot be underestimated by the environmentalists. Meanwhile on the international front the tide of events was surging powerfully behind those interests that stressed that national security was the paramount consideration in the energy field.

International Developments

By 17 October 1973 the Arab nations had threatened to cut oil production by at least 5 per cent immediately with further cuts until Israel withdrew from Arab territory and the rights of the Palestinian refugees were restored. A further threat developed to U.S. oil supplies when European nations moved to restrict exports of oil from the Middle East. By mid-October Italy and Spain were restricting oil exports and France, West Germany, Belgium and Holland were expected to do the same. The significance of this can be seen in the fact that around 17 per cent of U.S. daily oil consumption was at this time coming from Arab nations, either directly or indirectly as refined products, through Europe. In response to this manifest threat to the

American industrial structure the Administration and Congress battled fiercely over the best means to allocate oil and oil products during the expected winter shortage.

On 7 November the Administration seized an important initiative when the President announced in a nationwide broadcast a series of concrete measures to cope with the decreasing supply and increasing price of oil. First came six steps designed to curb U.S. consumption. They included (1) a bar on switching fuels from coal to oil; (2) reduction of fuel consumption for commercial aircraft (10 per cent reduction in flights) (3) reduction by 15 per cent in heating oil; (4) reduction of government energy consumption by 7 per cent; (5) speeding the licensing and construction of nuclear power plants by the AEC; and (6) reduction of the speed limit to 50 m.p.h. on highways. In addition the President took the opportunity to remind Congress to speed legislation relating to the energy problem. This included a four-point programme of (1) the trans-Alaska pipeline; (2) a Bill to encourage the production of natural gas; (3) the setting of reasonable standards for surface mining of coal; and (4) a set of structures to meet and administer energy programmes.

Backed by a mood of public concern to take drastic measures, the Congress responded rapidly. By 13 November, less than a week after the President's address to the nation, Congress had approved the immediate construction of the trans-Alaska pipeline. In terms of one of the major themes of this book — the emergence of self-sufficient superstates — one of the most significant aspects of the President's broadcast address was the unveiling of a package of measures which were labelled Project Independence.

Project Independence

Project Independence in reality brought together under a single programme umbrella a number of policies which had been evolving for some time. It also defines a crucial point in the evolution of those policies, at which security of supply, otherwise national security, was given top priority. By so doing the United States also recorded the almost unnoticed transition that had been going on from the most self-sufficient industrialised economy in the world to one which had latterly become significantly dependent on overseas suppliers. Since the United States has to think not only of her own security but of her role as a superpower and specifically her leadership of the Western alliance, these were changes akin to what some psychiatrists have described as the mid-life crisis, a time in their mid-thirties when hitherto vigorous people are reminded of their mortality and the limits to the achievement of their lifetime goals. That the United States, and more especially its industrial economy without which its much vaunted military capacity would be effectively impotent, had become in a real sense dependent was something of a shock to the American public consciousness. With considerable skill the Nixon Administration seized on the crisis mood to declare the need for a programme which invoked all the traditional virtues of self-support that had been first spawned in colonial America and the eighteenth-century achievement of independence.

By concentrating the nation's efforts on the exploitation of America's vast coal reserves, by deregulating natural gas, by bringing forward the nuclear power programme and the supply of oil from the Alaskan fields, the aim of Project Independence was to make the United States free from dependence on foreign energy sources by 1980. The project was compared with two other vast public projects which marshalled the resources of business and government to promote the public purpose the more swiftly, namely the Manhatten Project, which developed the atomic bomb, and more recently Project Apollo, which succeeded in planting a man on the moon in 1969. Though no price tag was given as to the extent of the financial resources made available, it was widely emphasised that more funds would be made available for the goal of energy self-sufficiency than were spent on the entire Manhattan Project. For the sceptically inclined this was less impressive than it might sound, especially when unofficial estimates put the funds earmarked for Project Independence as being about one tenth of the annual expenditure on space. Meanwhile Edward Symonds, Vice-President of the First National City Bank, estimated that there would need to be a total in the vicinity of 47 billion dollars of capital expenditure by 1980 to achieve self-sufficiency. As time passed, the date looked much more likely to be 1985 than 1980, with a corresponding growth in the expected expenditure. For the moment the goal was clear enough even if the time necessary to achieve it was suspected of being over-optimistic. But then much the same was true of the EEC's goal of monetary union — also by 1980.

At this point we will have to leave a detailed account of the course of the energy debate in the United States during 1974 to a more specialist study than this one in order to take up the narrative in 1975 when some of the public awareness of the urgency of the energy question had begun to wane as a variety of adjustments took place. As part of his effort to move the United States, and especially the U.S. Congress, to deal with energy issues, President Gerald Ford had proposed a plan to increase the cost of imported oil by three U.S. dollars per barrel. This was the President's chosen means of cutting consumption of oil, by increasing its cost. In the face of Congressional opposition in the shape of a Bill sent him by Congress on 19 February suspending his increase for 90 days, the President announced he intended to exercise his veto.

The imports likely to have been affected by such a Presidential measure were estimated to be about 4.1 million barrels per day of crude oil, 2.1 barrels of fuel oil and other refinery products. According to a report of the Senate Finance Committee of 17 February, the ripple effect of the Presidential proposals could cause a high inflation rate to be sustained throughout 1975 and also aggravate the general recession.

Decontrol of oil

Meanwhile, undeterred by congressional rejection of the increased import tariff on oil, President Ford announced his plans to decontrol the price of 'old' domestic oil as of 1 April (old oil is defined as that produced from wells existing in 1973 at a rate equal to 1972 production). The aim was to allow the price of old oil produced from wells in the United States to rise from the level of $5.25 per barrel, set in December 1973, to whatever price market forces determined. The existing controlled price was less than half the price of imported oil. The general intention was of course to stabilise domestic production. After decontrol the price of all oil would become standardised. A windfall profits tax was also urged by President Ford to ensure that the resulting price increases did not result in excessive profits for the oil companies.

Around the same time Congress was also weighing the future prospects of natural gas. Against the background of a serious shortfall in natural gas available and a declining rate of production, President Ford asked Congress to end twenty years of federal control on the prices paid at the wellhead for the United States' cheapest and cleanest fossil fuel. In the winter of 1974—5 the shortfall became so severe that it threatened layoffs in industries using natural gas and less directly imperilled food production by slowing the manufacture of fertiliser. Critics of deregulation argued that, in the absence of EPC controls, consumers would be left at the mercy of major oil companies which also happen to be the major producers of natural gas. Deregulation, the critics argued, would simply create windfall profits without guaranteeing that more gas would in fact be produced.

On the other side, favouring deregulation, the American Gas Association argued that

> natural gas is our dominant domestic energy resource. It provides one third of our nation's total energy requirements. However, when we eliminate oil imports and rely on home energy production, natural gas is our principal source of energy.

The Gas Association provided figures to demonstrate that natural gas constituted 41.1 per cent of total U.S. energy production, which significantly represented around 50 per cent of all energy consumed by U.S. industry. The latter statistic bore considerable weight with an administration increasingly preoccupied with future national security. The comparable domestic energy production percentage were 30 per cent for U.S. crude oil, 22 per cent for U.S. coal and a mere 6 per cent for current U.S. hydro and nuclear power.

Project Independence Report

On the subject of developing future new natural gas supplies the Project Independence˙Report was far from optimistic. Even with deregulation the Report anticipated that by 1985 gas production would have reached a level only slightly more than the current level which would be far below the potential requirements of the mid-1980s. Without deregulation, the

Report argued, gas production would taper off during the next decade to a point at which the gas shortage would become chronic enough to endanger the industrial infrastructure.

While the foregoing arguments tended to strengthen the convictions of the Ford Administration in favour of de-regulation, there were snags. Foremost among these snags was the fact, revealed by a Library of Congress study, that the annual cost of new gas deregulation would be roughly $5.5 billion. Meanwhile the two sides in the deregulation debate lined up predictably, with practically the entire energy industry favouring deregulation, including the American Petroleum Institute and the American Gas Association, respectively the lobbying arms of the major oil and gas companies, often synonomous; opposing deregulation were the consumer lobbies in the shape of the Consumer Federation of America and the American Public Gas Association. The crux of the gas industry's case rested on the argument that increasing the price was the only practical means of encouraging the production of increased supplies. Casting uncertainty on the calculations of both sets of protagonists was the claim of the National Research Council (a branch of the U.S. Academy of Sciences) that the Government's estimate of the reserves of natural gas, officially estimated at 2000 trillion cubic feet, was an overestimate and that a more accurate estimate was much nearer to 600 trillion cubic feet.

By the end of February 1975 President Ford had begun to lose patience with the Democratic Congress's inability to act on energy matters. On 26 February the President reiterated his request either to approve his energy Bill sent to Congress earlier in the year or to come up with an alternative energy Bill. The Democrats came up with a Bill of their own. It incorporated five major proposals designed to increase energy production with minimum hardship to the consumer.

These five features were: (1) a five cents per gallon increase in federal taxes on gasoline; (2) use of the proceeds from (1), estimated at around $5 billion annually, as an energy trust fund for alternative energy research and development; (3) a graduated tax on new automobiles with poor m.p.g. perfor-mances, with rebates for all those with consumption better than average; (4) the establishment of an independent advisory board called the National Production and Conservation Board; and (5) imposition of an excess profits tax on large oil companies.

Now that Congress had thrown off its lethargy and submitted proposals of its own, the prospect of some form of future compromise between the White House and Capitol Hill on a federal energy policy became a reasonable possibility.

Meanwhile on 12 March, in the continuing struggle between the environmental lobby and the producer lobbies, the Senate passed the Surface Mining Control and Reclamation Act of 1975. Against the historical background of the physical and social devastation of Appalachia from strip mining, the western states in particular with their vast mineral resources had increasingly combined to put a brake on untrammelled mineral extraction. The President having previously vetoed an earlier strip mining bill, the Senate made plans to draw up another bill to satisfy the demands of the Administration.

In approaching the point where a summary of U.S. energy policy, particularly in its external aspects, is called for, it is salutary to record the wide variation in domestic energy reserves estimated by the various national scientific organisations and industrial associations. The oil and gas reserves for the United States are given by three separate sources as follows:

	Oil reserves	*Gas reserves*
	(billion barrels)	(billion cubic feet)
U.S. Geological Survey	200–400	1000–2000
National Academy of Sciences	113	530
Oil companies	89	374

On the accuracy of these three respective estimates hinges the answer to the question whether the United States has domestic supplies of oil and gas to last sixty years (according to the U.S. Geological Survey) or only fifteen years (according to the oil companies). Such marked discrepancies in estimates only serve to underline the broad character of the estimates available.

Conclusions

The implications of U.S. energy policy, as we noted at the outset of this chapter, are global if only because the United States possesses both the most extensive range of sources of energy and the greatest pool of scientific skills to draw upon in the energy field. In addition we can reasonably deduce from the data employed to illustrate the domestic energy debate that U.S. energy policy has a profound effect on U.S. foreign policy, an effect likely to become even more marked in the future. For a variety of reasons which we will examine, the U.S. Government, by offering to share its technology and by pursuing a high-cost energy policy at home, has subordinated substantial technological advantages (and price advantages) in the energy field for the sake of broad political and diplomatic objectives.

Thus in setting a target of eliminating U.S. dependence on foreign energy within a ten to fifteen-year data, Project Independence implicitly accepted increased costs of about one third for consumers, possibly rising to half within the foreseeable future. At the same time the United States stressed the interdependent nature of the energy question within the industrialised world and the non-industrialised world too. In the words of Secretary of State Kissinger, 'No subject illustrates global interdependence better than energy.' This is still true. It was more true in 1973 and it will be less true as time goes on for the United States at least in the field of energy and raw materials. At the time of the first Arab embargo the United States faced the starkest form of shortage of resource requirements. Her daily imports of oil alone ran at about a million dollars. While this has been noticeably pruned, the United States continues to import vast quantities of vital raw materials. To illustrate this continuing dependence, it is estimated that three quarters of all the tin, platinum, nickel, cobalt, chromium, asbestos, manganese and bauxite consumed in the United States is imported. Yet the United States is much better placed than Japan or the European Economic Community. Moreover, this dependence is underlined by the fact that the United States, and the U.S. oil and nuclear power multinationals, need to maintain access to the major overseas markets for U.S. energy-related exports. Indeed, if Project Independence succeeds, the United States will become a net exporter of primary energy supplies. In addition, during the next decade the United States will almost certainly have so advanced its technology in the energy field that it will be willing to proffer its technology in the cause of interdependence, or alternatively and with less publicity, withhold its technology as a diplomatic bargaining counter. Already the United States has wooed in turn the EEC and Japan, the OPEC countries and the remaining oil importing countries, paying attention to their differing requirements and arguing for technological cooperation in the energy field, an approach which leaves the United States more dominant internationally than for quite some time. The primary forum for this energy diplomacy has been within the International Energy Agency, but a great deal is still conducted within the parent body, the OECD, especially within related fields such as raw material and monetary questions.

Like the chief organs of the Bretton Woods system, the International Energy Agency is very much an American creation to handle the post-1973 global energy issues. The United States needs on the one hand to provide a firm and creative leadership in the area of policy proposals but at the same time to avoid the impression of acting unilaterally. It is this inevitable U.S. dominance which has slowed the pace at which the eighteen oil-consuming nations have been prepared to surrender substantial powers to the IEA in the cause of making the emergency oil-sharing arrangements effective. While the U.S. Senate passed as early as mid-April (1975) the Standby Energy Authorities Act, bestowing on President Ford some of the emergency standby powers he had requested to deal with any future oil embargo, the majority of the members of the IEA had yet to pass any comparable legislation. Thus the two-phase emergency plan arose where the IEA relied on the oil multinationals to share out equitably available supplies among their subsidaries, followed by the possibility of further trading between the original oil subsidaries and other companies. To implement such a plan the IEA would be specifically empowered with the very widest of powers; this issue underlined the extent to which IEA members were being asked to delegate considerable sovereignty to an institution that was both American-inspired and dominated and gave extraordinary powers to the oil multinationals. But then the threat of a further oil shortage was extraordinary by any standards.

Meanwhile, within the United States, the increasing importance of the economic factor in international relations, of which energy and the related questions of monetary reform and raw material supply were vital ingredients, was beginning to be more widely recognised. This recongnition was clearly seen in the report of the Commission on the Organisation of the Government for the Conduct of Foreign Policy which, among its recommendations, urged the creation of a new senior post of Assistant to the President for International Economic Affairs whose main task would be to coordinate national and international economic policy. The Report registered its concern at what it saw as the lack of overall economic planning, noting in particular that the State Department was arguing for a guaranteed and high price (mainly, as we have seen, for reasons of national security) while the Treasury wanted the price of oil to be reduced. The report also recommended the appointment of more economists as ambassadors and moving the President's special representative for trade negotiations into the State Department.

While in the longer term the U.S. Government was pushing ahead by means of Project Independence to a position of self-sufficiency, in the short term she was seeking anxiously to create a directory of the Atlantic powers in consort with Japan to coordinate the crisis management measures on energy matters. By mid-1975, U.S. officials rated their major concern as whether the Western nations were in practical terms prepared to combine to the extent of presenting a united front ready to exercise an economic boycott against the OPEC countries and thus prevent the threatened 30 per cent increase in the price of oil the coming autumn. In addition, and flowing from the first fear, was·a growing American concern about the sale of nuclear energy reactors to the Third World countries. On the willingness and ability of the industrialised countries to abstain from selling nuclear reactors to countries so far without nuclear weapons hinged the future stability of the Middle East, to take only the most obvious example.

The possible failure of the industrialised countries to stand up to an oil price rise which might be as high as four dollars a barrel was, in the judgement of the Ford Administration, a very black cloud on the political horizon in mid-1975. If such a price rise should occur, the prospect of a recovery from the domestic recession in the United States would disappear instantly, while the consequences for the infinitely more vulnerable West European economy would be savage by constrast and the effect on the already weedy economic health of Italy, and most of all Britain, catastrophic. Holding such a pessimistic view the U.S. Government, unlike many European countries set very little store on commodity agreements as the means for stabilising relations between the industrialised and non-industrialised countries. The immediate U.S. expectations of OPEC however remained providentially unfulfilled.

Almost from the outset of the post-Yom Kippur war phase in international relations, U.S. external energy policy has been under-written by the principle to first bring about a reduction in oil prices through a united stand by the major consuming nations before entering into talks with the oil-producing states. The French have always sought to enter into dialogue with the producer states first and then hammer out some sort of accord between the consumer nations. Behind this approach lay first France's special relations with some of the oil-producing states such as Algeria, and second her unwillingness to accept a framework which placed the United States in a position of *primus inter pares* at the very least. Since the Martinique summit meeting between the French and American presidents and, near the end of 1975, the Rambouillet summit between the heads of government of the major industrialised nations, the French and American positions have moved significantly closer together in energy matters as in the related questions of world monetary arrangements. Further evidence of this was the December 1975 meeting between the oil-producing and the oil-consuming nations attended by both the United States and France.

The best summary statement of the U.S. position on external energy was made by Secretary of State Kissinger in an address to the University of Chicago. Dr Kissinger called for bold conservation efforts by the industrial nations which would embrace no further increase in the volume of energy imports over the next decade. The United States would aim to give a lead in this respect by reducing its energy imports from 7 million barrels a day to less than 1 million barrels. Dr Kissinger urged an international conservation agreement under which the industrialised countries would reduce oil consumption by 3 billion barrels by the end of 1975; the creation of a common fund by the International Energy Agency to finance or guarantee promising energy projects; the establishment by Japan, North America and Europe of a common loan and guarantee facility which would enable up to $2500 million to be redistributed in 1975 to finance oil deficits faced by oil-importing countries; the creation of a special trust fund

managed by the International Monetary Fund, to supplement
lending facilities to developing countries hit by the oil price
rises; and finally a meeting with the oil-producing countries,
which duly took place in December 1975.

Future US Energy Consumption

Since consumption in a high consumption nation like the
United States is as important a consideration as the extent of
the reserves, the following estimates for future consumption
assume added significance:

Estimated U.S. power consumption by source (U.S. Department
of Interior; U.S. Energy, the year 2000)

	1971 (per cent)	1980 (per cent)	1985 (per cent)	2000 (per cent)
Hydro-power	4	4.2	3.7	3.1
Nuclear power	0.6	7	10.1	25.7
Natural gas	32.9	28.1	24.3	17.7
Petroleum	44.2	43.9	43.5	37.2
Coal	18.2	16.8	18.4	16.3
Quadrillion BTUs	69	96	116.5	191.9

2 The European Economic Community

If the preeminent aim of the founding fathers of the EEC was political unification, the purpose of such economic instruments as the Common Agricultural Policy and the Economic and Monetary Union was always subordinate to the eventual political goal. Even earlier, both the ill-fated European Defence Community and the European Political Community provide examples of the Community's overreaching itself by attempting to consummate a premature form of political unification before either the political will or the common policy traditions had been established upon which any common political institutions could be built. Then in October 1973 came the painful moment of truth. After fifteen years of existence the Community faced an oil embargo. The common statement which it issued at the time must be regarded as the ultimate expression of a non-statement, indeed a confession of open division, that even the Community has issued on a topic of such vital importance to the survival of the Community's members. Some observers regard the sequence of events which transpired at that time to be the most abject expression of appeasement by a group of European nations since the late 1930s. Certainly without the intervention of the multinational oil companies the major component states of the Community would have stood aside while the Netherlands was deprived of essential oil supplies for not taking a sufficiently pro-Arab position.

The Washington energy conference held early in 1974 under the auspices of the Energy Cooperation Group served only to highlight the split between not only eight members of the Community and France but also between France and the United States, Japan, Canada and Norway on how to cope with the world energy problem. It is the open breach in the common front presented by the Community when the economic survival of its members was at stake that should not be dismissed too easily as an aberration when the proposals for common policies in the field of energy are analysed in this chapter.

By November 1974 the Energy Cooperation Group had developed into the International Energy Agency in the first instance to handle the urgent task of an oil-sharing programme which, as the Netherlands example illustrated, touched on the raw nerve of national economic survival as distinct from national self-interest. The United States got this programme off to a good start by formally pledging its own oil resources in any future embargo. For whatever the diplomatic denials to the contrary, the International Energy Agency was effectively a countervailing force to OPEC. It also represented rather less obviously but no less significantly an acceptance, at least for the meantime and on general principles, of American rather than French leadership. At the Martinique summit between the French and U.S. Presidents, the principle that the meeting of producers and consumers should be preceded by a consumers' meeting was first formally agreed. In the background U.S. policy remained to find a means of reducing the oil price.

Meanwhile the EEC Community Loan System began to evolve as a joint enterprise to provide medium-term loans with the oil-producing countries. Initially it was planned to have a borrowing arrangement of up to $3 billion, with a general procedure of relending the money to the central banks of the borrowing countries. To facilitate this arrangement, which became known unofficially as the Healey Plan after the British Chancellor who proposed it, there were further proposals to expand the facilities and membership of the International Monetary Fund, including direct contributions and voting rights for oil-producing states. The Healey Plan reflected the EEC disposition of bringing the oil producers into the energy crisis management system from the very beginning to play an active policy formulation role. This approach contrasted with the U.S. Government approach which favoured the prior consultation and organisation of the consumer countries to hammer out common policies before entering into negotiations with the producer states. The scepticism evinced by the U.S. Government over the prospect that a common front on energy might evolve among the industrialised countries in the process of bargaining with the oil producers was not without historical foundations. The record of the Six and later the Nine in evolving a common energy policy had been slow and tortuous.

EEC Common Energy Policy

The reasons for the slow progress of the Community in evolving a common energy policy are manifold, but three basic causes stand out. First, the responsibility for energy was divided: the Paris Treaty gave to the European Coal and Steel Community the responsibility for harmonising coal policy among the Six; the Rome Treaty laid down that oil, natural gas, electricity and hydro-power were the responsibility of the EEC Commission, while Euratom was delegated the task of coping with nuclear power resources. Such divided responsibility made it unlikely that a common energy policy to cover all three institutional spheres would develop without a great deal of conflict between the competing agencies. Secondly, in none of the three treaties which established the above-named bodies is there any mention of a common energy policy. The chief reason for this was that at the time when the Treaties were drafted in the early 1950s coal provided more than three quarters of the energy consumed by the Six. Arrangements to coordinate the remaining sources of energy were therefore of only marginal economic utility. The third reason why a common energy policy made such slow progress was that in order to come into being it would need to cut across a web of national mechanisms arising from the widely held precept that the regulation of energy was indispensable to the regulation of the national economy as a whole, not to mention its national security. In short, a common energy policy, by cutting across national policies in the field of energy producer monopolies, regional policy, nationalised industries and fiscal policy, was offering a challenge to sensitive areas in the anatomy of national sovereignty. Though less drastic in their implications than those of the proposals for economic and monetary union, the concept of a common energy policy was similarly conceived primarily to provide a *de facto* means of political unity rather than to rationalise energy policy among the Six and later the Nine. There were, however, more immediate practical forces that helped promote the drive towards a common energy policy.

Whereas in 1950 coal provided 75 per cent of the Community's energy requirements and oil around 10 per cent, by 1966 a dramatic change had taken place to the point where coal had fallen to 38 per cent while petroleum had risen to 45 per cent. These changes grew mostly out of an increase in the Community's industrial energy consumption and a demand for immediate cheap energy, mostly oil. This switch in energy sources was matched by serious social problems in the coal industry throughout Europe where among the Six the mining labour force below ground fell by 24 per cent and the number of pits by 42 per cent. The basic fact began to dawn on the Community planners that unlike the two other major economic blocs, the United States and the Soviet Union, the Community was already dependent on imported supplies of energy and was becoming increasingly so. This raised the question that we have traced in the previous chapter on the United States: how could stability and security of imported supplies of energy be maintained? Apart from temporary expedients such as stock-piling and diversifying oil supplies, it became clear that the only means of guaranteeing stability of energy supplies was by developing a common programme aimed at self-sufficiency. It is ironic to record that as far back as 1962, the West European coal producers and the British National Coal Board produced a joint report entitled *Meeting Europe's Energy Requirements* which warned that by the mid-1970s there would be a world[1] energy shortage and that it would therefore be prudent if the closing of mines could be halted. Within ten years its predictions were amply fulfilled, though its advice went substantially unheeded.

Meanwhile in 1964 the ECSC embarked on the beginnings of a common energy policy when the Council of Ministers formally adopted the Protocol of Agreement on energy policy, which laid down the very broadest kind of objectives such as cheapness and security of supply, fair conditions of competition among the various sources of energy and, not least, freedom of choice for consumers. Apart from coal, where a coordinated system of state subsidies was recommended, such objectives, by their lack of detail, illustrated the lack of real accord. Thus even the subsidies to national coal industries were to be provided by national exchequers. By the end of 1968 the Commission was ready for a further gradual step forward in the shape of a memorandum to the Council of Ministers entitled 'First Guidelines for a Community Energy Policy' (EEC Commission, 1968).[2] As in the Protocol the memorandum sought to reconcile the broad commercial objectives of freedom of choice for consumers and fair competition among suppliers with the strategic objectives of stability and security of supply.

Enlarging on the Protocol, the Commission memorandum of December 1968 urged that to meet the problem of national governmental distortion of demand the Rome Treaty be fully implemented. Thus within the Community complete freedom of movement of energy supplies should be a central ultimate objective. Some of the specific steps to eliminate national distortions are in the tax field: for example the harmonisation of the tax on value added in the energy sector, the harmonisation of specific consumer taxes on energy products and the harmonisation of taxes on hydrocarbon fuel. To achieve security of supply demands an entirely different set of measures.

The key to the growth of a self-sufficient domestic coal industry lies in coordinated import policy. Specifically, the Community's common commercial policy should set quantitative limits to coal imports. In the case of oil the Commission in fact persuaded the Council of Ministers to agree that member states should stock at least sixty-five days' consumption as purely national energy reserves to be commandeered by national governments in a crisis. In calling for a Community supply policy the Commission was trying, as diplomatically as possible, to draw attention to the pattern of oil imports and thus to promote a degree of diversification by Community-devised supply programmes. The Commission also recommended that the ECSC principle of drawing up forecasts of future demand should be extended from coal to all other sources of energy, not least to guarantee that investment is appropriately directed to meet such demand.

In addition, to secure competition in energy supply other than coal (where the Paris Treaty requires price lists to be published), the Commission proposed a notification system where major mergers were in prospect likely to provide an overdominant near-monopoly position in the supply of oil, natural gas and nuclear fuels. By the end of 1969 the Council of Ministers had approved the general outline as proposed by the Commission in their Memorandum of 1968.

By such gradual steps has progress been made in the elusive search for harmonisation of energy policy. If progress was tortuous among the Six for the first decade of the Community's existence, the enlargement of the Community to nine members meant the inclusion of Britain which, while it possessed substantial oil and natural gas reserves in the North Sea, also inherited a chronically weak economy. The future conflict between the overall interests of the Nine in energy and those of an economically weak but energy-rich Britain have thus long been evident. The nature and scope of the Community's energy pattern in both its productive and its consumptive aspects, to which the three newest members each had to adapt, needs examining as a first step to examining the development of a common energy policy from this point.

EEC Energy Patterns

The central role that energy plays in the industrial infrastructure and the social structures of the Six cannot be overestimated. The industries of the Six spent around one quarter of their annual budgets on investment in energy which amounted to about $25 000 million prior to 1973. In the iron and steel industry the proportion of investment was about 25 per cent; in chemicals, cement, ceramics, glass and non-ferrous metals, around 15 per cent; in the food industry, about 10 per cent. The companies engaged in the energy sector are themselves among the largest enterprises operating within the Community where they directly provide jobs for roughly one million workers and indirectly help create employment for many tens of millions. The availability of energy is a prime factor in the selection of industrial sites, and ultimately in the economic and social developments of particular regions. To give some perspective to this pattern of industrial energy consumption it must not be overlooked that energy (even before 1973) accounted for roughly one fifth of imports from outside the Community, or around $9000 million annually.

As the Community grew to consume more and more oil, her import dependence grew correspondingly. In 1950 the Six imported 13 per cent of their energy requirements; by 1960 the figure had grown to 30 per cent, and by 1970 to 63 per cent. In descending order (1970 figures) of energy dependence, Luxembourg was almost totally dependent on energy imports, while Belgium and Italy imported around 82 per cent of their energy,

France 71 per cent, West Germany 48 per cent and the Netherlands 42 per cent. Thus, over a twenty-year period, all the original EEC countries except the Netherlands (which discovered domestic sources of natural gas) have become increasingly dependent on outside sources of energy. Importing more than 95 per cent of the oil she consumed, the Community had by the turn of this decade become, at 580 million tce (tons coal equivalent), the world's largest crude oil market. The changing pattern of the EECs past, present and prospective (if unaltered) energy consumption can be seen in the following table:

EEC energy consumption: million tons of coal equivalent (mtce)

	1950	per cent	1970	per cent	1985	per cent
Coal	238.6	83	230.2	27	174	9
Oil	29.8	10	496.2	59	1304	65
Nuclear hydro	19.7	7	49.2	6	222	11
Natural gas	1.1	—	72.2	8	295	15
Total	289.2	100	847.8	100	1995	100

Apart from demonstrating the swing between 1950 and 1970 from coal to oil and prospectively towards natural gas, the above table does not take into account that from 1973 Britain (with great reserves of both oil and natural gas) joined the Community, nor of course the OPEC price rises following the October 1973 Middle East war. The increase in consumption of energy between 1950 and 1970 was spectacular. Taking 100 as the index for 1950 it rose by 1970 to 264 in the transport sector, to 257 in industry and to 358 in the household sector, the last reflecting the growth in household consumer demand or family living standards. Household consumption during this period increased to the point where it represented very nearly a third of total energy demand.

Pre-1973 EEC Energy Policy

As we have seen earlier in this chapter, the Community had great difficulty before 1973 in evolving a common energy policy, not only because responsibility for energy had historically been divided but for the even more basic reason that the different sources of energy were not of equal importance in each country. Thus Italy, the Netherlands and Luxembourg, for example, which had only small or non-existent coal outputs, favoured a cheap fuel policy which at this stage meant imported oil. By contrast, each of West Germany, France and Belgium argued for a policy of self-sufficiency, which in practice meant increased reliance on coal. Since three quarters of the Six's coal was mined in West Germany and a further 15 per cent in France, their position was readily comprehensible, more especially because ever since the early 1950s coal had become less price-competitive and was declining throughout the 1950s and 1960s at a compound rate of 2.1 per cent (over the same period the rate of decline in Britain was slightly higher at 2.35 per cent).

Nevertheless, whatever the long-term national interests of West Germany, France and Belgium may have been, the switch from coal to oil progressed almost unabated. As early as the time of the Suez crisis of 1956, when oil supplies were temporarily suspended, it was clear that oil had come to play an increasingly vital role in the Six's energy supply pattern. By 1964 it had overtaken coal as the chief source of energy, and by 1966 was providing more than half the Six's energy requirements. Indeed, it is true to say that oil accounted for almost all the additional demand for energy that arose between 1960 and 1970. All of this took place not because of any direct Community intervention in the shape of a common policy, but rather in response to the availability of oil in almost unlimited quantities and at very low prices. For a decade at least the Community consumer benefited from a supply of plentiful and cheap petroleum provided by multinational oil companies who were competing for the market of the richest oil importer in the world. It could not last. In October 1973 it came suddenly to an end which had long been anticipated in some form, but never quite so severely as it turned out in practice.

It was not unknown for the Community to make progress only in the face of a crisis; thus, when the Community responded to the energy crisis as we described at the beginning of this chapter, there was still some hope that the disarray that it caused would underline the need for concrete progress. By November 1973 the Commissioner responsible for energy seized his opportunity to urge forward the long-discussed plans for a common energy policy. Speaking to the European Parliament on 13 November, M. Simonet argued that the crisis arose from a 'structural disequilibrium between the supply of and the demand for petroleum'. The chief factors in that disequilibrium were the rapid increase in the consumption of petroleum, dependence on outside sources of supplies and rising production costs. The main purpose of the steps to be taken must be to achieve recognition of the common interests binding Europe and the producing countries.

M. Simonet felt that the chief lesson to be learned from the crisis was a political one; the problem of reliable supply for the Community and the diversification of energy sources had become a problem to be tackled directly by the governments of the Nine and the Commission. Such a statement, while it may not seem particularly original in the light of the narrative so far, represented implictly two very important developments in this field. Energy supply was now visibly so crucial to the survival of the member states of the Nine that it was absolutely essential for governments to regulate the supply directly, over and above the oil companies which had so far managed to retain control. In practice this was also an argument for the common energy policy which represented, if introduced, a joint intervention by the governments of the Nine. Secondly, Simonet's statement was a recognition of a *fait accompli*: that the Nine were heavily dependent on Middle East sources of supply (and would be for some time into the future) and would therefore need to develop strong political links. This is the first characteristic evidence of the superbloc as described in the earlier companion volume to this one, *The Politics of Trade*.

More specifically, Simonet's statement urged a stabilisation if not a cutting-back of the consumption of petroleum both to avoid actually running out and to give an opportunity of replacing oil with alternative energy sources. One of the chief objectives from now on in developing alternative sources was to attain a much greater measure of political independence. Simonet confirmed the priority which the Commission had recommended be given by the Council on 22 May, 1973 to the development of nuclear energy which must take the place of petroleum wherever possible. The nuclear sector, the Commission had stressed, should be developed both to provide independence from outside sources and as a means of cooperation in the energy field which incidentally lent itself to strict surveillance and control by government. If an extended programme of nuclear power stations were to be advanced, there had to be reliable sources of enriched uranium available in sufficient quantity. The Commission would shortly submit proposals to extend the Community's uranium enrichment capacity.

Last but not least of the Simonet proposals were those pertaining to a Community petroleum policy to handle the immediate crisis in both its monetary and its energy aspects. Three basic principles needed to be observed. First, a concerted programme of action had to be devised by the consumer countries; second, a programme of action between the consumer and producer countries had to be drawn up; and third, the oil market must be stabilised somehow, with the active collaboration of the oil companies.

In practice the Community's immediate response to the OPEC oil embargo and price rises was anything but concerted. Only three days after the Copenhagen summit of EEC heads of government, when a minimum agreement had been reached on an overall approach to energy, the Foreign Ministers of the Nine were deeply split. The occasion was an attempt by some member countries to bargain increased regional aid in return for cooperation in energy policy. Such stalling at a time when the need for concerted action on energy was desperate only served to underline the weakness of the current working methods of the Community.

While the Community was carrying out its normal procedures of trading off national advantages between the various economic and social sectors, the oil producers meeting in Teheran just before Christmas were receiving advice to raise the price from $3.10 per barrel to as high as $14. Though they settled in fact for half the latter figure, it was still enough to place the industrialised world in debt for some time to come, always assuming that such a price was maintained. It was now becoming apparent to most close observers that the issue was the enforced high cost rather than any absolute physical shortage. This was a basic truth that, as we have seen in an earlier chapter, the Americans had realised some time before; they had in consequence taken steps to bring the oil price under control even while the British, Italians and Irish were still blocking the drawing-up of a joint energy programme. Ironically enough, while the EEC had been anxious not to offend the

Arabs by presenting too united a front of consumers, it was the Americans that in fact brought this about first by means of the oil companies' lowering crude prices and then by bringing round all the EEC member states (except for the French) at the Washington energy conference. Despite the French barter agreement of arms for oil, an example followed later by the then British government on a smaller scale with Iran, the multilateral trading structure in the world oil market seems to have survived, at least with a handful of exceptions, for the meantine. France, West Germany and Britain in their respective ways have demonstrated their capacity to negotiate bilateral arrangements to safeguard their energy requirements. It is arguable that the very success of such bilateral arrangements in securing exclusive rights for their signatories undermines the possibility of a European energy policy for the future.

What is unarguable is that such deals were made against the background of the end of the United States' dominance of the international oil market. That dominance had consisted of the universal acceptance of the U.S. dollar as a world currency for oil payments, the provision by the United States of up to 50 per cent of the capital invested in the international oil industry, and not least the implicit and sometimes actual dependence on the U.S. indigenous oil industry as a reserve source of supply. It was the absence of the reserve U.S. oil supply (the United States was herself importing nearly 20 per cent) that differentiated the oil supply crisis of 1973–4 from the previous ones of 1956–7 and 1967. The new situation in the international oil market, and more precisely the end of U.S. dominance, left the EEC with the onus to respond to the changed circumstances with fresh proposals.

An EEC Energy Strategy, post-1973

By the middle of 1974 the Commission presented the Council with its first really comprehensive attempt to lay down the guidelines for a common energy policy for the following decade. In at least some senses the Commission's proposals were the EEC's equivalent to the Nixon Administration's Project Independence, although if the goal of self-sufficiency were common to both, the means to its attainment differed greatly. In the introductory section of the Bulletin of the European

Communities, Supplement 4/74, 'Towards a new energy policy strategy for the European Community',[3] it is pointedly emphasised that the main aims of the Community must be to create greater security of supply and to prevent violent changes in the price of energy materials. Three factors must be taken into the fullest consideration. First, the energy sources to be promoted must be available at the lowest possible price as an incentive to potential users; second, the producers have no interest in making the investments necessary for the future development of production if the profitability is too low; third, special attention should be given to the role the consumers can play, in particular how to make better use of energy resources which henceforth will be in generally much shorter supply and probably more expensive as well. The sudden and substantial increase in the price of imported crude oil also clearly raises issues that relate to the adaptation of the Community's national economic structures as a whole, not least in the short term the vast increase in the Nine's external debt. In the light of this the Community will need to respond to the energy crisis by not only redeploying the factors of production to meet the increased costs of energy but also increasing income from exports. Then comes the most telling if fairly obvious observation, that the scale of adjustments will differ widely between the member states of the Community. These differences embrace the balance of payments situation before the energy crisis, the scale of crude oil imports relative to total GNP, and the availability of alternative indigenous energy sources.

According to the Commission these differences are both valuable and hazardous to the Community.

> Valuable, because satisfactory cooperation among member countries would make for a fairer sharing of sacrifices over a period of time, to the benefit of the more exposed countries. Hazardous, because there is a danger that a difference in situations and prospects may lead to divergence in the policies and priorities of the individual member countries, the consequence of which would be to wipe out the potential advantages of a unified common market. To mitigate this risk, a Community strategy must be launched as soon as possible.

The Commission strategy envisaged two preeminent objectives above all others: the creation of a unified market for energy and the guaranteeing of security of supply — two very closely linked objectives. The assumption behind both objectives was that if such a common system works adequately in normal times it will survive the extra impact of a crisis, when its true worth becomes apparent.

In seeking to map out the likely course of events and especially the prospects for the supply of oil, the Commission in its 'Problems and resources of energy policy, 1975—1985' outlined two alternative hypotheses: first, that of a stable market with some surplus available, and second, that of a market where supply tightens, causing sharp price rises. Since the second hypothesis was thought to be more likely, and also because it demanded the greater degree of adaptation, it is the one we should examine in detail. The events of October 1973 and the embargo and price rises flowing from it make it crucial to the Community's survival that a reasonably correct prognosis is made on this very issue.

Four predictable consequences arise from the second hypothesis of shortage of supply and generally high prices. First, a slowing down in the increase of the demand for oil; second, the opening up of greater prospects for nuclear energy; third, a potential increase in the supply of natural gas; fourth, a more competitive coal industry and the prospect possibly of even importing coal from outside the boundaries of the Nine. The overriding need in such circumstances — that is, those of continued reliance for the meantime on imported energy materials — is security of supply, which means diversification so that neither the quantity nor the price can be put at risk by the political action of a major supplier.

The core of the Commission's energy supply structure for the long term — that is, for 2000 — rests on two major components, nuclear energy and gas. The Commission believes that the advantages of nuclear energy — its ready availability, adaptability, ease of transport and storage (including its 'presumed' protection of the environment) — outweigh its disadvantages which are itemised as lying in the realm of the limits to technology, environment, sites, waste products, financial capacity for investment, industrial capacity, and so forth. The weakness of the nuclear energy priority argument is that the precise

consequences of the massive production of nuclear energy are
not yet fully explored, especially its hazards to the environment, not least to man himself. Such is the priority given to
security of supply that the Commission confidently envisages
that by the year 2000 at least half the total energy requirements
within the Community could be met by nuclear energy. As the
Commission admits, such an objective requires the guaranteeing
of stable sources of supply of uranium ore, a commodity
essential to nuclear energy and in short supply within the
Community. Again there is the need for conscious coordination
of the Community's links with the producers of uranium and
the systematic diversification of uranium ore supplies — if only
to avert the erection of a cartel — a theme touched on in the
very brief Postscript.

The gas obtained from a variety of primary sources (be it
natural gas produced in the Community or imported from
outside, or synthesis gas from oil or solid fuels) might by 2000
account for nearly one-third of energy consumption. Besides its
own inherent advantages, mostly as the cleanest form of energy,
gas offers in the longer term the additional recommendation
that it is also an outlet for nuclear energy. Thus the infrastructure for transporting gas could gradually be used for
distributing hydrogen or synthesis gas produced by nuclear
means. The interconnection of the nuclear and gas energy
sources as a means of providing sure supplies of energy thirty
years hence has as part of its purpose to leave the Community
only minimally dependent on non-renewable resources such as
coal and oil, of which the latter is strategically very vulnerable.
It also assumes that the non-conventional energies such as solar
and geothermal energy would be playing an increasing role,
leaving coal and oil to meet something under a quarter of the
Community's total energy needs.

All of the preceding long-term aims would depend upon their
fulfilment on a very large number of preconditions, of which
the following three might be regarded as crucial. First, the
required action needed to be taken immediately, not least
because if the technological problems were to be overcome the
energy research and development programmes had to be
substantially stepped up. Second, whatever action was embarked upon, it had to provide solutions for the short and

medium-term problems as well as the longer term. At the same time it had to be a framework which would allow rapid modification to meet a sudden change in the availability of respective energy sources. Third, and a point on which some scepticism might be in order as to the extent of the Commission's convictions in their order of priorities, full account must be taken of the need to preserve the natural environment and improve the quality of life. So much for the long-term objectives and guiding principles; we must now devote our attention to the much shorter term, specifically the objectives for 1985.

EEC Commission, Energy 1985

Any Community energy policy for the next decade has to be based on certain assumptions or basic hypotheses as to future trends. It is useful initially to examine four basic factors as they have been assessed by the Commission:

(1) The rate of growth: prior to 1973 the Community's GNP had been predicted to increase at an average annual rate of 5 per cent. Taking account of the admission of Britain and the effects of the 1973 Middle East war, this prediction was lowered to a rate of 4.5 per cent, which may well be an overestimate but avoids the dangers of underestimating energy demand.

(2) Substitution and its effect on demand: the new post-1973 price relativities between the various energy sources will bring about changes in demand for almost all of them. There are nevertheless, the Commission assumes, a series of constraints that operate to minimise the changes that certain consumer sectors might otherwise make. Thus both the iron and steel industry and motor transport offer little flexibility in demand, whereas the production of electricity can be based on a number of different fuels. It is interesting that in this respect the EEC Commission adopts a far more conservative stance than the contemporary U.S. Administration, which has consciously sought to lower motor transport consumption through both the price mechanism and the tax structure.

(3) Rigidities in supply: some sources of energy will have to be gone ahead with for one or other of two major reasons — either because the investment has to be based on long-term

prospects of profitability (such as North Sea oil and natural gas, and even new coal mines) or because they are by-products of certain production processes (such as coke-oven gas or refinery gas).

(4) Investment: despite the staggering post-1973 increase in oil prices, the future prices for any particular substitute for oil are still unpredictable. The only prudent investment strategy must set out to increase the flexibility of demand, at the same time developing those sources of supply having the maximum flexibility. In so far as it is technically possible, investment should be based on energy with a high degree of security of supply, with the balance to be covered from more uncertain sources.

Energy Balance Sheet, 1985 Targets

On the demand side:

(1) The implementation of a deliberate policy to obtain a more efficient use of energy, reinforced by the effects of the price rises, should make it possible to reduce by one percentage point the average rate of annual increase in requirements between 1973 and 1985 without in any way reducing the economic and social product obtained by means of the energy consumed. Total energy consumption would then be approximately 10 per cent lower than the figure originally envisaged.

(2) While avoiding an increase in dependence on oil, electricity consumption must be raised from 25 to 35 per cent in order to establish the largest possible market for nuclear energy. This expansion of electricity must be sufficiently gradual to first stabilise and then reduce the consumption of petroleum products in power stations.

On the supply side:

(3) Nuclear facilities would be increased and could cover half the production of electricity from the middle of the 1980s. The possible extension of nuclear power to the production of industrial heat should not be eliminated. By 1985 it might be possible to have a total available capacity of more than 200 GW.

(4) Solid fuel consumption must increase, making use of both domestic production, which will have to be stabilised at the present level, and imported coal.

(5) The high potential demand for natural gas must be met by an increased supply (both from within the Community and from outside) while maintaining the lowest possible price and security of supply.

(6) Oil consumption must be concentrated on specific uses such as motor fuel and for certain applications as a raw material. The more efficient use of energy would gradually lead to an end to the increase in crude oil requirements, so that by the mid-1980s they might be held at a level barely higher than 1973, after a slackening growth rate continuing until around 1978/80. By 1980 the availability of North Sea oil and natural gas will have reduced the dependence of the Community on outside suppliers to some considerable extent, but it raises what is a crucial political issue in the whole energy policy sector.

Imported Energy Dependence

Unlike the United States, which is comparatively rich in energy resources, the European Economic Community cannot adopt the aim of energy independence as a medium-term objective. Nevertheless it must in the medium term greatly increase the security of its imported supplies, a necessity which greatly influences its political links with the Middle East countries.

Meanwhile the policies just set out would, if adopted, make it possible to reduce the share of imported energy in total consumption from around 60 to about 40 per cent. These are approximate estimates, if only because even indigenous energy production cannot be regarded as totally secure if it is not commercially extractable. Moreover, the indigenous energy proportion is calculated on the basis of nuclear energy generated from imported fissile materials.

Investments and Budgetary Costs

The foregoing Community post-1973 strategy can be characterised by a striking increased reliance on Community production, notably from the North Sea and from the accelerated expansion of the nuclear sector. The immediate question is, can the Community spare such a switch of investment to a long-term nuclear programme when the demand for industrial investment in the short-term is so pressing? The true alternatives are whether the Community, in the face of the need to safeguard energy supplies, should invest more for indigenous energy production or invest more for export and the purchase of both energy and raw materials. In either case there should be a slowdown in real consumption.

The following are the likely costs in terms of investment if the foregoing strategy proposed by the Commission were to be adopted:

(1) Cumulative investment in the energy sector as a whole, in the period 1975—85, would be approximately 300 000 million 1973 dollars.

(2) A major proportion of this would be absorbed by electricity, with total expenditure of the order of 150—180 000 million 1973 dollars, including $120 000 million in the nuclear sector.

(3) In the hydrocarbons sector, where the figures are subject to the greatest uncertainty, it can be assumed that the emphasis placed on Community gas and oil and some decline in investment in refineries would result in expenditure of the order of 110 000 million 1973 dollars.

(4) Maintaining the output of solid fuels should account for around $6000 million.

Thus, summarising the investment sector, whereas it accounted for some 1.5 per cent of the Community product in the period 1965—70, the figure will probably be between 2 and 2.5 per cent for the period 1975—85. Thus the additional investment might be as high as 1 per cent of the gross Community product. Obviously, the requirements of member states differ widely both because of the discrepancy between their economic strength and because of the pattern of their energy structures. The need to develop a form of political solidarity which will enable appropriate compromises to be made needs no underlining.

As a rough approximation, the proposed Commission energy strategy during the period 1975—85 requires an extra investment effort of around $10 000 million. However, underlining the gain in security of supply, it also represents a net economy to the balance of payments of around $50 000 million during the same period. Assuming that the prices of oil and natural gas remain comparatively high (and without any competitive alternative energy, that is a near certainty), the additional investment that the Commission's strategy recommends is significantly smaller than the scale of increased exports that the Community would be obliged to engineer to offset the cost of hydrocarbon imports. Moreover, the additional investment in the nuclear sector affects only power stations and permits lower investment in oil refining. The escalating costs of the exploitation of North Sea oil to the British are a reminder that these are not merely macro-economic decisions, and any energy framework must provide the incentive to risk capital.

Indeed, the Community's policy towards pricing and indirect taxation is a crucial element in the exploitation of indigenous energy, as the debate between the Ford Administration and the U.S. Congress in 1975 testifies. In Europe there is a need for a prices policy offering conditions for the adequate long-term profitability of investments which are designed to attain the original commercial objective. Thus such factors as incentives to speed up investments, fiscal aids for energy sources with a high initial cost as well as structures to facilitate the raising of loans on the international capital market all need to be incorporated in any Community energy strategy. But in order to develop a coherent Community energy supply policy for the next decade there has to be a serious implementation of such a policy for *each* source of energy, resulting in both incentives and curbs in the administrative and financial fields. Such politicisation of energy, recorded at this point in the book merely to be catalogued, would need to be carried out at both the Community and the national member state levels, if it is to be effective. Since there is such a conflict of interest not only between the various nation states but also between the various energy sectors seeking preferential treatment, there would need to be a sustained pattern of cooperation or such a fundamental strengthening of the Community's powers in the energy field that collaboration was imposed.

The four chief sources of energy upon which the Commission feels that the Community should concentrate its efforts are those of, first, electricity and nuclear energy; second, coal; third, oil; and fourth, natural gas. Since the concentration on nuclear energy as one of the leading sources involves a major switch in emphasis and the most significant reallocation of financial and human resources, it will be examined before those of the more conventional hydrocarbon sources of energy.

Electricity and Nuclear Energy

The crux of the advantage of electricity over its energy competitors lies in its price and its security of supply. This can be appreciated when it is remembered that the cost of fuel for conventional power stations represents approximately one third of the final cost of electricity to the consumer. With the growth of the share of nuclear energy, for which the fuel cost is still lower, the effect of the cost of fossil fuels on the price of electricity will decrease. Electricity is also a reliable form of energy, not least because it can be produced from a wide variety of sources ranging from nuclear fission to hydro-power.

Evidence of the increasing demand for electricity can be seen in the fact that during the decade from 1965 to 1975, the average annual rate of increase in demand for electricity has been 7.2 per cent in the nine Community countries, which represents a doubling in demand every ten years. Most of this increased demand is likely to be absorbed by heating and transport.

But the Commission warns that this increased demand for electricity, which already exists, must be met not by increased dependence on petroleum products as it has been hitherto, but by a stepping-up of nuclear energy supply. The trouble is, as the Commission readily acknowledges, that it is not possible to contemplate a higher rate of increase for the next five years. Only from about 1980 onwards will the full effects of the substitution of electricity for petroleum products (mostly from nuclear plants) become felt. By 1985 it is conceivable that electricity's share in primary energy consumption will have reached 35 per cent, as compared with around 25 per cent in the mid-1970s. By 1985–90 the annual rate of increase in the production of electricity could, if the Commission's proposals were adopted and consistently implemented, reach a figure of 9 per cent.

In order to achieve such a boost to the use of electricity it would also be essential to deploy the energy available from present power stations more rationally — that is, if an adequate return is to be obtained on the huge sums of capital likely to be invested. Constancy of demand during the day, week and year lies at the heart of the cost effectiveness of nuclear power stations, a point which has not been lost on the Russians in their construction of a national electrical grid, described in the next chapter. A better distribution of consumption, particularly by industrial consumers, can be greatly aided by appropriate pricing measures to encourage consumption outside peak hours.

Meanwhile conventional energy sources for electricity generation are likely to remain essential until 1985 at the earliest. These include brown coal (notably in West Germany), hydro-electric production (though there are estimated to be few sites unexploited with sufficient head of water), manufactured gas and other by-products which will tend to expand at roughly the same rate as the industry producing these fuels without any need for intervention by the Commission or member governments.

Above all, coal itself will have to fill an increasing stop-gap role in electricity production, since in the next ten years the production of coal-fired power stations is capable of being increased by up to 50 per cent, always assuming that the coal is available at a commercial price. In fact coal has now, for the first time for some years, reached a level of competitiveness with petroleum. Bearing in mind the fluctuations in the past, and the time it takes to bring even old coal fields back into production, such theoretical competitiveness is not in itself enough. If coal is to be substantially utilised in the production of electricity over the next decade, long-term contracts will need to be drawn up between the coal producers and the electricity producers.

Nuclear Energy

In this most controversial of the major sources of energy a basic distinction needs to be made between the long term on the one hand and the short and medium term on the other, with beyond 1985 qualifying as the long term. In the long term, up to and beyond the year 2000, nuclear energy is likely to become the preeminent source of energy arising from fast breeder reactors and fusion devices which generate electricity, process heat, gasify coal, produce both synthetic gas and hydrogen – in fact satisfy the majority of an industrial society's requirements, however omnivorous. Such is the scientific possibility and the planners' vision for the future. Meanwhile there is the short and medium-term future with its multiple problems to be solved.

Even between 1985 and the end of the century, the importance
of the aforementioned developments may be strictly limited in
their immediate application. What is much more certain is that
in the short and medium term the chief role of nuclear energy
will be to provide an alternative form of energy for producing
electricity. Its function will be to produce electricity which
cannot be obtained from 'inevitable' or privileged fuels — such
as industrial gases, hydro-electricity, geothermal sources of
power, brown coal, and so on — and requires a high load factor.

All of the nuclear energy strategy thus outlined is designed to
ensure that by the mid-1980s, 50 per cent of electricity
production is likely to be nuclear-based. Specifically, this
percentage represents an installed capacity of at least 200 GW in
1985, to which could be added the production of process
steam, which in 1985 could be equivalent to an annual
consumption of about 25 million tonnes. However, to attain the
foregoing nuclear production targets certain problems are
acknowledged by the Commission as needing to be overcome.

These problems hinge on three chief concerns: first, the
capacity and, in times of recession, the commitment of the
Community's industries to build the required power stations in
the required time; second, and probably of the greatest concern
(certainly the Commission is noticeably reticent about providing reassurance to qualified objections in this sphere) is that
of ensuring that the development of nuclear energy does not
harm either public health or the environment. The Commission
has already taken steps to carry out

> forward analysis of the potential radiological implications of
> nuclear construction programmes over a period of 25 years,
> together with the adaptation of basic standards of health
> protection in the transport of radioactive materials, the
> recording and storage of radioactive wastes and the safety of
> nuclear installations.[4]

All this may be reassuring up to a point, but the simple fact of
increasing nuclear production and thus multiplying nuclear
wastes manifestly increases the chances of human error, to say
nothing of terrorism or any irrational use of such diabolical
destructive as well as creative power in times of either peace or
war.

Third, and from a strategic viewpoint most significantly,

there is the problem of supply of nuclear fuels to power plants. The Community currently has strictly limited supplies of natural uranium to draw upon and will remain a net importer of enrichment services of one sort or another for the next decade at least. In the case of natural uranium a very thorough investigation of the means of maintaining stable relations with suppliers was undertaken by the Commission which singled out the crucial suppliers. In the field of enriched uranium the Commission has already made proposals concerning the creation of uranium enrichment capacity on a European-scale, an undertaking whose costs would need to have a thorough public airing if it were ever embarked upon with any great seriousness. The concept of dangers to public health enters into the argument in the nuclear field, adding reinforcement to the general fear that energy policy involves gigantic and expanded public and private investment long before the mass of citizens have any idea what is happening.

Coal

One of the more obvious consequences of the October 1973 increase in oil prices is that much of the Community's coal production has now become competitive with other fossil fuels. However, having been systematically run down through most countries of the Community for so many years in the long period when oil prices were uniformly low, the coal industry is hardly ideally placed to take advantage of this unfamiliar situation. The time it takes to develop new productive capacity, to recruit and train new manpower, to attract substantial long-term investment with all the uncertainty in the energy sector – all these factors make the possibilities of a rapid turnabout difficult, always assuming the political will exists in the first place. The demand for coal nevertheless seems more dependable than for many years.

For one thing, taken together power stations and the steel industry absorb around 80 per cent of Community coal consumption, of which nine tenths are produced in the Community. Since steel-making has proved itself less than well adapted to switching to new fuels, the likelihood is that coal consumption by the steel industry (accounting for about 40 per cent of total coal consumption) will remain steady. Conventional power stations are likely to remain coal-fired.

Coal: EEC Production Objectives

If the Commission's target of maintaining coal production at its present level (at least) of around 250 million tonnes is to be achieved, certain basic conditions have to be fulfilled, of which the following head the list.

First, there must be a geographical rationalisation of the coal industry by concentrating production in regions with high or potentially high industrial productivity. Wherever this rationalisation policy is overruled for reasons of high unemployment, with no immediate alternative industries demanding labour, the temporary maintenance costs should be borne by the 'appropriate' authority which has made the decision to make an exception, be it the Community, the national or the regional government.

Second, the Community must press ahead with measures to support the existing mines deemed well placed and open up new mines where they offer a commercial future. Such measures will include loans through the European Investment Bank and possibly other low-interest loans through Community resources.

Third, a manpower policy must be adopted throughout the Community which stimulates the recruitment and training of highly skilled labour by means of attractive wage levels and secure career prospects, also giving financial incentives to provide labour mobility.

Fourth, a price policy should be adopted which is directed towards the attainment of a free market situation where coal from one country can compete unhindered against coal from another, as also between coal and other forms of energy.

Fifth, a financial contribution should be made by the Community to intensify research and development work towards the improvement of working conditions, to which no-one could object. But the Commission also adds, rather euphemistically, that such research should be for 'the reduction of the impact of labour costs and production', in other words the reduction of the labour force. While the goal of maintaining the present level of coal production is spelled out in detail, the Commission is not so foolish as to spell out that it would also intend to achieve this with a greatly slimmed-down labour force. Without debating the wisdom of such a policy, there is a recurring tendency in Commission documents to dodge the harder aspects of the policies proposed. At the same time there is a sidelong acknowledgement by the Commission of the political difficulties of running down the coal labour force in its advocacy, admittedly in the most general terms, of financial support to guarantee the competitiveness of coal to consumers who have long-term contracts to buy Community coal, also financial stimuli to promote coal-fired power stations and the consumption of coal in the electricity sector.

Whatever degree of intervention the Community finally settles for, and whatever level of coal production it is able to maintain, what is fairly safe to predict is that there will be a need for increasing quantities of imported coal from outside the Community. The general principle that the Commission favours in the light of the expanded market potential for coal in the EEC is that long-term contracts with foreign coal producers should take the form of joint-venture mining operations. Apart from the Iberian peninsular, one of the chief areas from which coal is likely to be imported is Eastern Europe (see the next chapter, on the Soviet Union). The key aspects therefore to be watched in the future coal import policy of the Community lie in its role of supplementing internal production and being subject to monitoring for the prospects of security of supply. As part of the overall strategy to stabilise conditions of supply for coal, both internally and externally, the Commission urges a policy of stockpiling in the hands of both producers and major consumers, to anticipate any interruption in the free flow of coal or of any other energy for that matter. The interrelated character of energy supplies cannot be overemphasised and provides one of the chief justifications for an overall energy coordination strategy, given that the Community is likely to require an ever greater supply of energy overall in the years ahead.

Oil

Of all the major sources of energy, oil has been the subject, at least since 1973, of the most acute public awareness. The Western industrial system, with its enormous appetite for cheap fuel, has been around for so long that the public in most Western societies is still inclined to adopt the short-term solution rather than the more rational long-term one. This principle is as much evidenced by the obduracy of Congress in blocking President Ford's efforts to raise the price of domestic oil (by an act of decontrolling it), in order to restrain consumption and provide incentives for exploration, as by the absence of almost any legal restraint (by means of the price mechanism) on oil consumption in Britain. Meanwhile, from an examination of the skeleton of the Commission's proposals for an oil policy, several factors stand out:

(1) Oil remains an essential main element in the Community's energy supply pattern. The chief reason for this is that demand for oil is likely to grow substantially during the period of time necessary to develop the replacement energy sources. Even though if the Commission's strategy is carried out and the Community's oil consumption drops from 61 per cent of total energy consumption in 1973 to 41 per cent by 1985, oil will still represent the main single source of energy for the Community.

(2) Oil worldwide has come under much stricter control by the producer countries, notably the OPEC states, with consequent long-term uncertainty in terms of both price and security of supply.

(3) New oil deposits will come under flow both within the Community (chiefly in the British North Sea oilfields) and in contiguous regions (i.e. the Norwegian North Sea oilfields). This will gradually have the effect of reducing the Community's dependence on its traditional oil suppliers in the Middle East, North and West Africa.

(4) The part played by multinational oil companies, while still integral to the exploitation of oil resources generally, is coming under considerable modification in its structures and processes. This is most markedly apparent in the fields of marketing and finance.

(5) The oil requirements of other consumers worldwide will exert a growing effect on the world market for oil upon which the Community will have to depend for the next decade at least. As the survey of other major consumers in other chapters in this book makes clear, it is this very interdependence by the

major oil consumers, the dependence on the producer states as well as the interrelated character of the industrial economies, that the major industrial powers are anxious to break.

Any Community oil supply policy policy must take account of the foregoing circumstances if it is to succeed in its basic objectives: as with the other major energy sources, a balance between stability and security of supply without sacrificing the prospects of a reasonable economic growth rate for the next decade or more. In pursuance of such a basic objective, the Community's oil supply policy for the next decade, as recommended by the Commission, rests on four major planks: (1) a common policy towards oil-importing and exporting countries; (2) the development of secure resources; (3) Community machinery making it possible to take appropriate measures to deal with supply difficulties; and (4) the organisation of the proper functioning of the market at Community level.

(1) Relations with the producer and consumer countries

Within three months of the October 1973 Middle East conflict the Commission, with admirable promptness, submitted to the Council proposals[5] on the Community's relations with the producer countries. In practice these proposals were almost unanimously ignored, most notably by first France, then Britain and later West Germany who proceeded to negotiate bilateral deals with the major oil-producing states. Far from involving mutual consultation, such bilateral deals were not only conceived as safeguarding the national energy interests of the European state concerned but sometimes positively discriminated against a member state of the Community. As the Commission sees it, energy policy should be regarded as merely an aspect of a common trade policy. There is more than a slight hint of exasperation in the tone of the Commission's request for a decision on a common policy position by the Council towards the producer states. As subsequent events were to reveal, France, not for the first time, had ideas of its own which prevented a common front emerging. Much of the same thing applied in the case of the consuming countries collaborating within the structure of the OECD. On the one hand the Commission urged the application of the full provisions of the

Rome Treaty in regard to the negotiations and the adoption of a common position; on the other France was determined to take up a stand different from that of the United States, the more so when it perceived that the United States was using the oil price rise crisis to rally the Western industrial states to follow its leadership within the forum of the OECD. Somewhat forlornly the Commission urged the Community to speak with a single voice within such bodies as the OECD, 'so proving the existence of an indispensable European identity'. Lacking France's support the other eight members of the Community joined hands with the remaining principal Western industrial nations to create the International Energy Agency, underlining the common threat to the industrial economies of the major oil-consuming states and more than incidentally the division of approach among the members of the Community.

(2) *The development of secure resources*

The Commission foresaw, as did most other observers, that a concerted effort was needed to encourage prospecting and production of oil in new areas. The financial cost of this development should be borne by the oil industry, though the Commission believes that the Community can sometimes play an active part, citing that between the 1974 and 1976 budgetary estimates of the Community, 25 million units of account have been allotted annually for this purpose. The Commission urges that such an allocation be increased, though it is worth noting that in the most productive source of Community energy supplies for the future, the North Sea, private enterprise has sustained the entire development cost.

Up to now the Community's support for energy development has been confined to technological development in the hydrocarbons sector, but the Commission would like to extend its direct involvement to prospecting, storage and transport sectors. The chief motivation for this expansion of direct Community participation in energy development is, in the words of the Commission, 'to provide a Community incentive' to forge links between the multinational oil companies contributing to the Community's supplies. Here we have the familiar motivation of forging yet another means of political collaboration as the chief end in view to which the commercial objective of cheaper oil is a subsidiary question. Such links — that is, structural and financial links between the energy multinationals — naturally serve to reinforce the bureaucratic links between the Commission and the multinationals.

(3) Measures to deal with supply difficulties

There are, in the Commission's view, two major purposes lying behind all Community measures in this field: to maintain the freest possible circulation of all sources of energy within the Community, and to moderate the effects of any shortfall in supplies overall. The unpalatable truth is that both these objectives are more easily recommended or even legislated than achieved.

Long before the oil price rises following the October 1973 Middle East war, there were Community provisions in this field. They included Council Directives of 20 December 1968 (imposing an obligation on Member States of the EEC to maintain minimum stocks of crude oil and/or petroleum products) and of 19 December 1972 (requiring much the same thing), yet they proved inadequate to the challenge. From this disappointing experience the Commission realised that it was necessary to create a framework for the Community incorporating an information and monitoring system, a range of measures to reduce consumption quickly by all member states and, not least, coordinated action in the realm of price agreements.

All these measures could be administered at national government level but would benefit from conforming to overall policy guidelines established at Community level on the basis of Commission proposals. The general objective in creating such a framework was to make it possible to act rapidly and with the maximum degree of flexibility when the next crisis occurred. Some acknowledgement that the coordination of international energy policy could not afford to ignore the wider framework of the OECD can be seen from time to time in passing references by the Commission to OECD decisions and principles.

*(4) The organisation (at Community level) of the proper func-
tioning of the market*

As the free flow of goods in general is indispensable to the
proper functioning of the customs union, so the free circulation
of energy is essential to an effective Community oil supply
policy based on shared sources of information and concerted
action. The supply of information revealing the quantity and
value of both imports and exports, investments, and the cost
and price of petroleum products, should be made available,
according to the Commission, in order to introduce some degree
of standardisation.

Specifically the Commission recommends the provision of
regular information to a standardised pattern showing the various
prices and cost elements for crude oil and oil products imported
into the Community. From these the Commission argues that
there should be quarterly fixes giving some indicator of the
average level of the cost of supplies. The Commission also
believes that it is desirable to have a detailed analysis of the
costs of refining and distribution operations in each member
state. Clearly, the Commission subscribes to the principle that a
comprehensive knowledge of the facts is the first step to
exercising a degree of control in such matters as energy.

The principle which the Commission sees as essential to the
proper functioning of the market on a Community-wide basis is
what it calls a 'flexible system of concertation' which it sees as
being carried out by the Council of Ministers, the member
states, the EEC's Committee of Energy and the companies
which supply the Community. As the Commission has repeatedly declared (in terms which confirm the corporatist characteristics described in the Introduction):

> it is appropriate to associate the directors of these companies
> with the deliberations of the public authorities, by means of
> concertation. The purpose is, by initiating a dialogue which
> will provide the conditions for the smooth evolution of the
> views of all parties concerned, to preserve — and to bring into
> play gradually — a pattern of behaviour which, while respect-
> ing the Treaty rules, takes due account of the public interest
> and the legitimate aims of the industry. . . .

The Commission goes on to add that this concertation should
take place in the Energy Committee.

Concertation Principles   The concertation procedure envisaged by the Commission embraces the agreement on such questions of supply as the annual forecast of imports, five-year importing plans (or alternatively long-term supply contracts for indigenous fuel), the financial terms of supply, the manner of handling shortages when they arise and the means of ensuring the security of supply; also the effective regulation of the Community market by providing investment forecasts, by plotting distribution patterns of the available quantities of crude oil and oil products, by deploying the necessary technical and financial resources for stable and sufficient energy supplies and by generally ensuring a system of equal competition between the various sources of supply. As is apparent, the preceding areas of 'concertation' embrace the whole spectrum of energy policy for the simple reason that if the Community cannot exercise a degree of control over energy, as it notably failed to do in 1973, then its influence over the pattern of the Community's industrial pattern for the future and its overall ability to create closer collaboration between member states will remain seriously suspect.

Bearing closely in mind the Community fiasco over oil in 1973–4, the Commission recommended in mid-1974 that a much more hard and fast Community oil policy be drawn up which, to be effective, needed as back-up the full compliance of member states in the field of competition policy, common commercial policy and differing price levels. For all these reasons the Commission favours a greater degree of uniformity (this does not imply standard prices) in these price levels rather than in the price structures. Such a goal, the Commission observes cautiously, can only be achieved by gradual stages. The first step would be to encourage consultations between the member states and the Commission before any decision is taken to alter prices; the second step would be to harmonise progressively the criteria underlying the price structures applied to determine the level of prices; the third and final step would be to establish a Community system based on the publication and availability of prices. Within such a structure the parties to long-term supply arrangements should be allowed to fix their prices freely. The Commission nevertheless, significantly, wishes to reserve for itself the power to intervene when there develop either movements of a speculative nature or any other policy likely to undermine the Community's overall energy objectives.

Natural Gas

Although natural gas is regarded as a very subsidiary energy source compared with petroleum, it already accounts for around 12 per cent of the Community's total energy supply; by 1985 it could, it is estimated, account for more than double that proportion, or almost 25 per cent of the Community's requirements. Such a doubling of the share provided by natural gas is based on certain broad assumptions, such as the doubling of Community output in ten years and the increasing future reliance on energy imports compatible with the aims of security of supply.

Since its exploitation is usually closely linked with oil, and the major oil companies are effectively the major natural gas companies too, the Community's general approach to natural gas is seen by the Commission to require a broadly similar policy and set of basic principles. Thus, to increase available supplies of natural gas it will be essential to intensify prospecting in the Community. According to the Commission this will require, first, the provision of precise information, presented in a standard pattern to the public authorities, on the reserves of natural gas existing within the Community and, quite as relevant, the prospect of working them; second, the possibility of taking administrative and/or fiscal measures to encourage prospecting for new deposits, and even of granting financial aid in the form of a strictly controlled Community projects system; third, encouraging the conclusion of new contracts or the extension of existing contracts for the import of natural gas with Third Countries, and eventually through the conclusion of Community trade cooperation agreements. Clearly the third method of securing a supply of natural gas involves dependence on outside sources of supply, which seems to cut across the principles of self-sufficiency outlined previously. Nevertheless, on the whole, natural gas imports tend to be more secure than oil imports; moreover they also further diversify the origins of supply.

Storage and Transport

Crucial to any Community role in the supply of natural gas is an enlargement and integration of the transport and storage system. Such a Community role would be chiefly preoccupied with increasing safety standards by common regulations, with achieving a better coverage of the seasonal variations in the increasing demand from the highly varied regions of the Community, and not least with strengthening the security of supply. The most obvious means of expressing such a strategy would be Community regulations governing gas pipelines, transport and storage facilities generally. At least this is the approach that naturally recommends itself to the Commission who believe that in order to optimise the economic use of natural gas the mechanism of the market is by itself insufficient. Thus, according to the Commission, the use of natural gas in new thermal power stations should be made subject to arrangements requiring prior authorisation in order to keep fuel for applications where it can be used to better advantage. The Commission goes on to suggest that it will be necessary to promote the general introduction of contracts which can be interrupted in respect of large industrial consumers wishing to run on natural gas. Whatever the rights or wrongs of such regulatory proposals by the Commission, they represent graphically the extent of control that the Commission means to assert in the future. To underline its determination to establish control over the Community's energy policy in very practical terms, the Commission stresses that a harmonised policy of prices and price scales at Community level will require a high degree of 'transparency' if natural gas is to be utilised 'in conformity with Community energy policy'.

Conclusions on EEC Strategy

Whatever the particular merit or demerit of the specific proposals which make up the Commission's proposed energy strategy, they pose two quite fundamental problems: to create the appropriate instruments to implement such policies, and to establish relationships between prices in conformity with these guidelines.

The first problem implies a necessity for action throughout the whole energy sector. This might extend to prospecting for, exploiting and marketing new resources located inside or outside the Community; the participation of Community firms in joint ventures; the development of the necessary infrastructure (transport, stocking facilities, etc.); research and development into new means of producing energy or more effective means of using it — all within a framework likely to protect the environment. None of this proposed intervention must conflict with existing common policies already introduced by the Community in other sectors, or if they threaten to do so they must be administratively reconciled at the highest level in the Commission.

The second problem, that of divergent, disorganised price movements arising from instability of the market, would of course completely nullify the whole strategy envisaged by the Commission. Not only would such price movements hinder the attainment of the objectives of the Community's energy policy, but they would also put at risk vast sums of capital invested to achieve those Community objectives. Another risk would be the recreation of barriers in the energy market between member states of the Nine. A joint approach to Community energy prices in general is indispensable to any future common energy policy.

Conclusion

The energy sector is, even within the Community, a vital one employing in all about two million people, accounting for about one quarter of total industrial investment and representing six per cent of the production costs of other branches. Should a Community common energy policy on the scale envisaged by the Commission become law, it would have vast internal ramifications for the nature of the West European industrial economy and the scope and scale of Community institutions.

In addition, and of particular interest to the general theme of this book, there are vast external ramifications. Until the discovery of major oil and natural gas deposits in the North Sea, the Community of Nine managed to produce only about 2 per cent of its requirements for crude petroleum. Since the North Sea is only now coming into substantial production the Community remains the largest importer of crude petroleum, purchasing almost one quarter of world production or about half the international trade in crude petroleum. Two regions, the Middle East with 64 per cent and Africa with 30 per cent, account for almost all the Community's imported crude oil.

In turn, the Community accounts for 40 per cent of the Middle East's crude petroleum production and 62 per cent of

Africa's crude oil, underlining the very close links which bind the Community with the Eurafrican hemisphere. In 1972 the principal suppliers of crude oil to the Community in order of importance were Saudi Arabia (23 per cent of imports), Kuwait (14 per cent), Libya (14 per cent), Iran (11 per cent), and Nigeria (9 per cent). By and large these countries have remained the principal suppliers of the Community up until the present day. Equally, despite major plans for diversification of energy, the European strategy on petroleum up until 1973 has been to transport the raw material from non-Community countries and to refine it at the place of consumption. Thus the Community has the greatest refining capacity in the world, about 25 per cent of global capacity. Since 1973 the Arab oil states have drawn up plans to greatly enlarge their refining capacity in their own countries, at or near the oil fields, and thus encourage the tanker trade to switch from transporting crude oil to the refined product.

As we saw earlier in this chapter the EEC, despite the privations of 1973, only managed to take its first major practical step towards oil and fuel sharing in December 1974, more than a year after the energy crisis had come to a head. Nothing illustrates more clearly the inescapable fact that of the five superstates the EEC is the most tenuously held together — not withstanding that, because of its global diplomatic and commercial connections, a legacy of the ex-imperial role of its chief members, its influence is among the most pervasive even when it lacks any coherent overall global pattern. Meanwhile the December 1974 decision of the EEC Council of Ministers was to agree a package of conservation and energy diversification measures which, though modest by the standards of some other superstates, was at least a concerted programme of joint energy measures upon which agreement had finally been reached. If fully implemented, these measures could reduce projected Community energy consumption by 15 per cent and reduce dependence on external supplies from 63 per cent in 1973 to between 40 and 50 per cent by 1985.

The framework in which EEC energy proposals have been drawn up is one which incorporates a broad energy programme for the next twenty-five years and a more detailed immediate programme for the next decade, not unlike, in its two-tier aspect, that of the United States. While the principal objective

Total energy requirements[a] of the European Community in 1973 and 1985

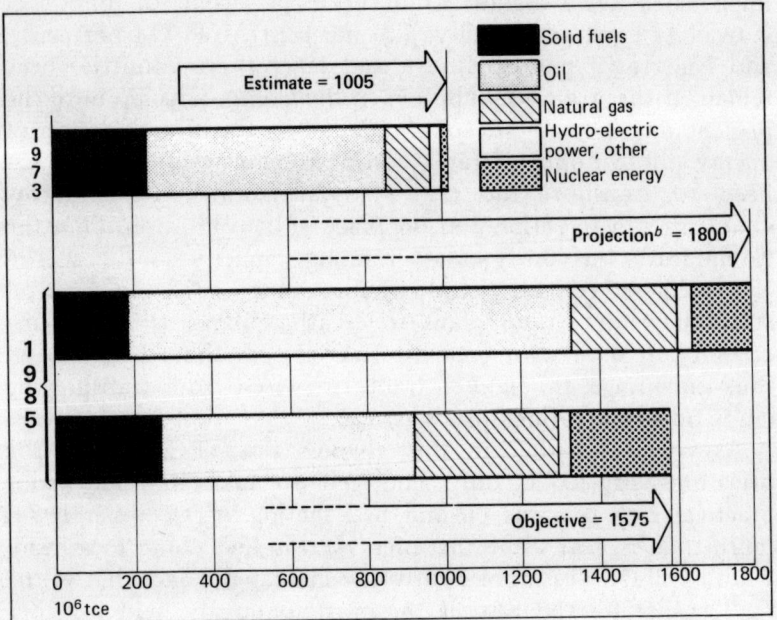

a: Internal consumption + exports + bunkers
b: Based on market conditions in late 1972

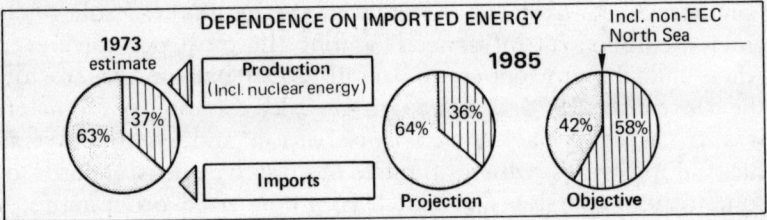

Source: 'Towards a New Energy Policy Strategy for the European Community' (June 1974) p. 16.

of both short and long-range programmes is to reduce dependence on imported oil through an intensive development of nuclear power and greater use of coal and gas, the Community's future chances of greater self-sufficiency hinge to a very great extent on the success of British energy policy and especially the rate of development of Britain's North Sea oil and natural gas deposits. It is not for nothing that Britain sought separate representation from the Community at the December 1975 oil producer–consumer conference.

With the possibility that by 1980 Britain might be providing 90 per cent of the Community's oil and possibly 45 per cent of its total production of energy, Britain has expended a greater proportion of its gross national product in energy production than any other member of the Community. With the prospect of national self-sufficiency by the early 1980s from its North Sea oilfields, Britain has been understandably anxious to press on with the process of oil and gas development and limit any intervention by the Community to an absolute minimum. Its scepticism about the possibilities of developing a comprehensive EEC energy policy, and an equal degree of scepticism about the possibilities of fashioning an effective common approach among the consumer and producer countries, highlight its special position within the Community.

3 The Soviet Union

Despite the ushering in of a new era in international and commercial relations between the two superpowers following the accords between the United States and the Soviet Union of May 1972, the dispositions of the Soviet military establishment and the direction and content of Soviet foreign policy remain a primary factor in the rationale of American national security, and indeed for the national security policies of much of the rest of the world. Within this framework energy policy is a very central issue. But before energy policy can be usefully examined the overall and comparative performance of the Soviet economy needs outlining.

Although the Soviet economy in terms of its gross national product is only half as big as that of the United States, it nevertheless continues to allocate a comparable absolute amount of goods and services for military, space and aid programmes. Fully conscious of this gap in productivity between the Soviet Union and the United States, the Soviet Ninth Five Year Plan (1971—75) underlined the importance of technological improvement by means of closer commercial ties with the West. This Soviet awareness of its competitive deficiencies in relation to the economic performance of the United States can be dated from about 1972, when the Soviet gross national product rose by about 2 per cent at a time when the Western economies were by and large experiencing boom conditions. The spectacular failures in agriculture in this period were the more disastrous since Soviet agriculture still accounts for about 25 per cent of GNP. Soviet dependence on foreign technology imports was painfully underscored while the 1972 grain sales had the effect of drastically curtailing the growth of such imports. Apart from chemicals, trucks and computers, this dependence on foreign technology was nowhere more acute than in the technology of the oil and gas industries whose deficiencies we can examine later in greater detail.

As long as Soviet military expenditure was rising in real terms by 4 per cent per annum, and around 16 per cent of Soviet non-agricultural labour (one third of the total labour force being deployed in agriculture) was employed by the military establishment, one might reasonably argue that the Soviet economic performance would continue to lag behind the United States. The possibility of a partial demobilisation of military manpower in order to attain specified economic goals first became a serious option in the early 1970s. It may indeed have partially accounted for the noticeable thawing in Soviet attitudes in the SALT and MBFR talks about this time. Another factor which came into play in the early 1970s was the Soviet shortage of hard currency. Throughout the 1960s right up until 1971, the Soviet trade deficit with the West had run at around $300 million per annum (it topped $600 million in 1972). This was financed by Soviet gold sales, a situation which because of the diminishing of a capital asset could not continue indefinitely. Since 1972, therefore, the Soviet Union's continuing deficit with the West, which at one time reached $3 billion, has been underwritten by medium and long-term credit guarantees by Western governments.

Thus, according to John P. Hardt in his summary essay in *Soviet Economic Policy for the 1970s* (a compendium compiled for a joint Committee of the U.S. Congress), if the Soviet Union is to achieve its stated economic goals it will need to modify its present economic policies in three main areas: (1) by reducing military expenditure and making it possible to transfer military skills more readily to the civilian sector; (2) by improving planning and management; and (3) by expanding commercial relations with developed nations to facilitate the acquisition of Western technology.

Meanwhile each of the superpowers has an interest in the other's economic prosperity. As the United States is likely to need the Soviet Union's raw materials, especially oil and natural gas, for some time to come, so the Soviet Union needs both American technology (particularly energy technology) and feedstuffs (especially high-protein feeds). In terms of the likely balance sheet between the two superpowers, the benefits to the United States of a close commercial partnership at this stage are likely to accrue in the form of a billion-dollar income from U.S. manufactures exported to the Soviet Union. These exports in turn can be calculated to provide somewhere around 60 000 extra jobs for U.S. workers. The benefits to the Soviet Union of trading with the United States are closely tied up with size. The Soviet Union likes big projects, bigger than most European and Japanese firms like making. Thus when it comes to barter deals U.S. companies have a built-in advantage over their Western rival companies in treating with the Russians. This advantage is accentuated by the fact that the United States and the Eurocurrency market together constitute the largest credit pool. Nor should the fact that the Soviet Union regards its commercial partnership with the United States as an aspect of her superpower status be lightly dismissed. Such things mean more to the leaders of a relatively closed society than is fully appreciated in the West. The fact that the Soviet Union, with a late start in the industrial stakes, actually produces more oil, coal, steel, glass, cement and machine tools than does the United States is a point of considerable and justifiable pride of attainment, even though total output is half that of the U.S. economy and consumer output only a third.

The most striking aspect of recent Soviet economic development is that for the first forty years Soviet planners left Siberia outside their calculations, but since the surfacing of the Sino-Soviet conflict in the late 1950s, and especially since March 1964 when Mao laid claim to a great tract of Soviet territory, Siberia has been a top priority for both internal investment and more lately (since the discovery of great raw material and energy resources) foreign joint investment ventures. This Siberian development has been spurred on not only by the Chinese threat but also by even broader strategic requirements (which the Soviet military leaders have been quite explicit about) to pursue a policy of industrial dispersion wherever it could be reconciled with reasonable economic criteria. Thus the Soviet Defence Minister, Marshal Greko, wrote authoritatively on this theme as follows:

> The movement of production forces to the East, bringing them closer to the sources of raw material and fuel and their dispersed location by economic districts significantly raises the defence capability of the Soviet homeland and makes our industry less vulnerable in the event that the imperialists initiate a missile-nuclear war.

However forcefully or moderately the so-called Siberian policy is pursued by the Soviet leadership in the years to come, there can be little doubt that it represents the greatest treasure house of Soviet energy and raw material resources, to that extent it provides the key to the Soviet supply and demand outlook for energy, an outlook which has worldwide ramifications for at least four basic reasons. First, the Soviet Union is the possessor of a large share of global energy resources; second, it possesses an advanced technology for fuel production; third, it is a major and increasingly important consumer of energy; and fourth, it is one of the chief participants in world trade in energy resources. For all these reasons the course of Soviet energy policy has immense significance.

An Account of Energy Developments in the 1970s

During 1974 the Soviet Union became the world's largest producer of oil, its crude oil production reaching 3400 million barrels, or around 200 million more barrels than the United States. Against the background of Western reports that the Soviet Union was likely to suffer from a serious energy shortage in the near future, it is useful to examine carefully the official Soviet claims and weigh them against the most reliable of the externally compiled estimates. If the United States estimates of total energy reserves should (as we have seen in chapter 1) vary widely according to the estimating body, it is hardly surprising that there should be differences as to the extent of the Soviet Union's energy reserves and its capacity to exploit them fast enough to meet an acknowledged growth in energy demand.

According to Alexander Nekrasov, chief energy expert of the USSR Academy of Sciences' Institute of Economics and Mathematics, the Soviet Union has the biggest mineral fuel resources in the world. By the mid-1960s Soviet oil resources already prospected were sufficient to supply the Soviet Union for several decades. Since then a vast new oil-bearing area in Western Siberia has been discovered and has now become the biggest oil-bearing area in the entire country. Moreover, according to Nekrasov, the Soviet Union accounts for one third of all global deposits holding promise of oil and gas. Most of the foregoing is not in serious dispute.

The argument about the extent of possible Soviet energy shortages in the near future arises because of the relatively low level of current exploitation of the selfsame oil and natural gas deposits which for the most part are heavily concentrated in Siberia and the northern part of the Soviet Union. It is because of the uneven distribution of its energy resources, 90 per cent of which lie in the Asian section, that the Soviet government has found it convenient to import fuel and energy into some areas in the eastern part of the country. Supplies of natural gas to the Transcaucasian republics from Iran are a notable example. For the moment there cannot be much doubt that the Soviet Union is self-sufficient in energy generally, since it exports around five times more than it imports. This is not to say that it does not wish to maintain and develop close commercial relations with the oil-rich states lying to the south-west of European Soviet Russia, if only for strategic reasons, that is, to deny to the Western powers the prerogatives of any exclusive relationship. But it is doubtful whether the Soviet Union needs these sources for its current energy needs. How long it can maintain a high degree of self-sufficiency in the face of increasing energy consumption and the inaccessibility of much of its own energy resources is the nub of the question which we can examine critically later in this chapter.

Meanwhile the optimistic forecasts of Soviet geologists, who besides claiming one third of the world's oil and gas-bearing strata also claim 55 per cent of the world's coal reserves, together with the vast and far from fully exploited hydro-power from the Soviet Union's extensive river system, have encouraged Soviet planners to allow for a rapid increase in energy consumption. Indeed, by the year 2000, the total production of fuel in the Soviet Union will have grown fourfold since the mid-1970s and may have reached as much as 6000 million reference tons (i.e. the 1970 figure for world consumption, predicted by the Soviet government to rise to 20 000 million tons or more by 2000). Unsurprisingly, the Soviet establishment makes a show of confidence not only about the steady growth in both consumption and production of energy but also about the superiority of the Soviet long-term planning system over that of the capitalist countries. It is undeniable that, when the Western countries are operating their mixed economies with alarmingly high rates of inflation, unemployment and volatile energy price fluctuations, the efficacy of central planning, especially in the energy field, becomes increasingly attractive.

COMECON'S History

In January 1974, against the background of considerable disorganisation and loss of confidence among Western countries in the wake of the OPEC price rises and selective embargo, the Council for Mutual Economic Assistance celebrated its twenty-fifth anniversary. Back in January 1949, representatives of the governments of Bulgaria, Czechoslovakia, Hungary, Poland, Romania and the Soviet Union met in Moscow to create the first international economic organisation of Communist countries. By turn, the German Democratic Republic was to join the Council in 1950, Mongolia in 1962 and Cuba in 1972. In essence it has remained a Soviet-dominated Eastern European bloc with its two newest members admitted for the sake of bolstering their precariously exposed positions in both an economic and a political context.

Its economic achievements have certainly been considerable in the industrial sector, where output has increased by 740 per cent; by contrast agricultural output has lagged behind, increasing by a mere 120 per cent in the same twenty-five year period. Nevertheless the Comecon countries, representing 10 per cent of the world's total population now account for 33 per cent of world industrial output compared with around 18 per cent in 1950. Thus the conventional military superiority that the Soviet bloc has possessed over NATO since 1950 is now supported by a substantially stronger economic infrastructure.

Soviet Energy, post-1973

Although the Soviet Union has not undergone the pervasive economic crisis which emerged out of the OPEC price rises, for the obvious reason that the OPEC states constitute a currently marginal source of Soviet energy supplies, nevertheless it has drawn its own conclusions and is more than ever determined to create a comprehensive self-sufficiency in energy for the future when energy demand will have noticeably increased on mid-1970 levels. In this respect the pattern of response in terms of energy diversification and priorities bears striking similarities to the two previous energy policies we have discussed so far – those of the United States and of the European Economic Community.

Oil Despite the existence of gigantic indigenous reserves of both oil and natural gas, as already described, the Soviet government has planned its future energy balance with a striking expansion of coal mining, nuclear power and hydro-energy. However, as the Soviet Union is the largest single producer of oil in the world, we should first devote our attention to its oil policy. There are around six major locations where very substantial oil reserves have been identified: they range from the island of Sakhalin in the Far East to Byelorussia, from Western Siberia to Central Asia, and from the north of the European part of the country to the south of the Urals. Of all these, the West Siberian fields are regarded as having the greatest potential.

In Western Siberia oil exploration and development have been extremely hazardous because of the harsh nature of the terrain, the forests of the taiga and marshlands, not to mention the rigorous climate. Thus it took oilmen around seven years to extract the first 100 million tons of oil and only a year and a half to obtain the second 100 million tons. With more than sixty separate deposits already known to exist, the plan is to extract some 300 million tons annually by 1980 (this compares with a total Soviet production of 450 million tons in 1974).

Western Siberia is also rich in natural gas. Soviet geologists have estimated that natural gas deposits in the Tyumen region amount to 60 per cent of the nation's total gas resources. By the mid-1980s the Soviet energy planners hope that it will become the Soviet Union's chief supplier of natural gas. The Urengoy deposits alone are believed to contain five billion cubic metres of gas lying under a permanent frost within the Arctic Circle (this compares with 250 million cubic metres of gas as the current Soviet total output). Yet all these reserves of gas and oil lie beneath a boundless taiga, marshes and innumerable lakes that presented a major challenge to the engineering resourcefulness of Soviet oilmen. They responded by laying down a network of highways spanning the marshes and creating entirely new towns at Nizhne Vartovsk, Surgut, Neftevugansk and Strezhevoy. Major pipelines already link the Siberian fields with the Ural and Volga areas and with the central industrial regions of the European part of the Soviet Union. Altogether somewhere around 42 000 kilometres of main pipelines were laid in the four years 1970—4, underlining the rapid tempo of Soviet

oil exploration which in Western Siberia was in 1974 about one
year ahead of its Five Year Plan target for drilling. Siberian oil
has now received (via pipeline) an outlet to the Soviet Black Sea
ports, while gas pipelines link the gasfields of the northern parts
of the Soviet Union with Byelorussia and the Soviet Baltic
republics. The development of this enormous network of
pipelines is not without great strategic significance for the
Soviet navy's Baltic and Black Sea fleets. But there is also a less
obvious overall development taking place, with even greater
strategic implications.

One of the striking things about the great developments
taking place in the West Siberian plain is that, because they are
taking place at great distances from the oil-refining and
oil-consuming centres, they necessitate major capital investments for the total development of the surrounding areas. This
is being embarked upon quite willingly since it represents a
conscious policy objective, namely the beginnings of a major
population movement in the Soviet Union from the western
republics to the vast underpopulated hinterland of Siberia.

According to Professor Boris Khorev, a leading Soviet
demographer, the movement of the Soviet population to the
east is now very substantial, and the trend is accelerating. At
this moment about 90 per cent of the total population of the
Soviet Union — around 253 million — live in what has generally
been regarded as the European, western republics. But with the
growth in energy consumption arising from the growing
industrial strength of the Soviet Union there is some pressure to
create fresh industrial complexes closer to the sources of
available energy. Since around 90 per cent of the country's fuel
and power resources lie in the east, there is a natural inclination
to stimulate the migration of people to man the new economic
expansion there. Moreover, the industrial requirements also
accord with the strategic importance of creating centres of
industrial power as far as possible from the Soviet borders — be
they European or be they Chinese.

A number of direct and indirect means have been deployed
by the Soviet government to promote both the industrial
development and the movement of suitably skilled migrants.
First, as we have already described, there was the magnet of the
big new industrial complexes arising from the oil, gas and
forestry resources of the West Siberian plain. By the end of

1974 the West Siberian oil fields were producing more than a
third of total Soviet oil production. Second, the current
construction of the Baikal—Amur railway (linked to the
trans-Siberian railway), running for 3200 kilometres, was
conceived as a powerful stimulus to the economic development
of Siberia and the Soviet Far East, a territory bigger than all
Europe, into which the Soviet government plans to move a
million people. Third, as a direct incentive to attract new
settlers to the east, the wage coefficient rises as the climate
becomes harsher. Thus the oilmen of Western Siberia are paid
70 per cent more than those in the European part of the Soviet
Union. The government also provides grants to families of
settlers, together with free transport of families and their
possessions to the designated place of settlement. Most ex-
travagant of all, by comparison with the incentives familiar to
regional aid recipients in the EEC countries, new settlers are not
required to pay rent or to pay for communal services for two
years after moving, and they pay no income tax for eight years!

Coal Western Siberia's energy resources are not, however,
confined to oil and natural gas. The Raspadskaya mine in the
Kuznetsk coal fields of Western Siberia, opened in late 1973, is
expected to become the largest single coal mine in the entire
Soviet Union. By the end of 1975 total Soviet coal production
was predicted to reach the 700 million ton mark. Most of this is
used to produce electricity and for coking. Through chemical
treatment it is also used to obtain coal tars, plastics, fertilisers,
drugs, gas and liquid fuels. It is also used for heating purposes,
particularly in the rural areas.

    While the country's oldest coal fields lie in the Kuznetsk and
Donetsk basins in the Ukraine, where new coal faces are still
being opened, the major expansion in coal mining is certain to
occur in the east where mining can be carried out on a large
scale. For although the extraction of the most valuable coal is
still carried out underground, a switch to the opencast method
is becoming widespread in the east. By the end of 1975 very
nearly one third of all Soviet coal was being extracted from
opencast mines, with no impediment from any environmental
lobby to contend with as in the United States. Because of the
low investment required and the scope for using powerful
machinery, opencast coal is not only competitive with oil and

natural gas but in some circumstances can substantially under-
cut them. Nearly all the most promising deposits for opencast
mining are in the eastern parts of the Soviet Union, and the
largest are the Bogatyr deposits at Ekibastus (Republic of
Kazakhstan) which, it is anticipated, will eventually produce up
to 50 million tons a year.

In the last few years over a hundred deposits of coal
have been discovered on the steppes of Kazakhstan, containing
an estimated 160 000 million tons. The Turgai field alone has
reserves estimated at 60 000 million tons. Most encouragingly,
the Turgai coal lies within only 200–500 kilometres of the
great power stations of the Urals. By Soviet standards this is a
relatively short distance when one considers some of the
resources which lie untapped in the eastern part of the country.
By the year 2000, Soviet scientists estimate that Kazakhstan
will be producing about 250 million tons of coal annually.
Much of this will then be consumed locally in thermal power
stations which will provide cheap electricity to be carried by
high-voltage power transmission lines to the Urals and to the
central parts of the Soviet Union.

But it is not only in Western Siberia that vast coal and
industrial development plans are being set in motion. The USSR
State Planning Committee had already begun in 1974 to draw
up plans for a big power and industrial complex to be developed
in Eastern Siberia over the period from 1976 to 1990. These
plans included the construction of thermal power stations and
the creation of energy-intensive industries linked to the
Kansk–Achinsk coal basin. This basin stretches for 700
kilometres (over 430 miles) along the trans-Siberian railway
with seams of coal sometimes up to 60 metres thick. Preliminary estimates suggest that total reserves may exceed
1 200 000 million tons.

Nuclear Power The Soviet Minister of Power and Electrification, Pyotr Neporozhny, said in 1974 that atomic power
stations would introduce new capacity totalling 30 million
kilowatts within the next ten to twelve years. During the Ninth
Five Year Plan (1971–5) something like seven million kilowatts
were added to total capacity, chiefly through the building of
one million kilowatt power stations.

Among the most crucial projects in the efficient utilisation of

Soviet power in the next decade is the introduction of a unified national power grid linking the present eleven power grid systems. It has been estimated that it is possible to save 35—40 million kilowatts by switching electricity from one zone to another in accordance with the times of peak demand. The target for total Soviet power production by 1980 was 1 500 000 million kilowatt-hours or 330 million kilowatts

An Analysis of Energy, post-1975

After a preliminary analysis of the overall direction of the Soviet economy, we have now completed a brief account of the development of Soviet energy resources up until the present. Since the subject is of global significance, and since for the sake of security there is an inherent temptation to obfuscate the issues, a more detailed scrutiny of Soviet claims is necessary. The critical analysis of Soviet energy policy and its likely future direction in the next decade which follows is an attempt to sift the evidence, though without reaching firm conclusions when the evidence is incomplete or contradictory, as it most often is in this most hotly debated of national energy policies.

Reserves

There can be little doubt that the Soviet Union is richly endowed with reserves of each of the traditional energy sources such as oil, gas, coal and water power.[1] It has also great reserves of low-grade energy sources such as peat, shale and firewood which, while they are being steadily supplanted by more efficient fuels, exist as a back-up domestic energy source. For the future, however, the trend is increasingly towards the use of oil and gas, rather than as in the United States, away from them. Also in contrast to the United States, where the environmental lobby has secured increasing restraints on strip--mined coal, in the Soviet Union it is fast becoming the most important form of solid fuel, not least because of its accessibility by comparison with a great deal of Soviet energy reserves.

With reserves of at least 18 trillion cubic metres, the Soviet Union's reserves of natural gas are the largest in the world. This means that reserves of gas stand at about 80 times current annual output. Most of this can be put to one side until foreign capital is available for its extraction. Soviet reserves of coal are also colossal, something of the order of 311 billion tons (excluding brown coal), and at the moment highly competitive from a comparative cost viewpoint.

Soviet oil reserves are less easily and precisely calculated for the simple reason that they cannot be fully disclosed under the Soviet state secret act. There is nevertheless no doubt that Soviet oil reserves are quite immense. They fall into two distinct areas in the west and east respectively.

In the west the discovery during the 1950s of large sources of oil in the Volga–Ural region was the basis for the Soviet industrial expansion of the 1960s. However, what now seems to be happening is that these fields are declining rapidly in oil output. The cost of exploration and development of some of the smaller fields is proving prohibitive, while the actual output from the smaller fields is much lower than the Five Year Plan anticipated. Thus there has been a general falling away in the productivity of the older established Soviet oilfields in the west, a trend which has been at the heart of the Soviet concern about oil supplies in the mid to late 1970s.

Meanwhile, fortunately for the Russians, in the east there has been a welter of major discoveries in Western Siberia, western Kazakhstan (Mangyshlak) and less dramatically in Byelorussia and some of the older areas in the west. It is from the east, therefore, that most of the future expansion in Soviet oil output will derive, as we have already implied in the account of recent exploration. From this exploration it is now clear that half of Soviet explored reserves lie in this eastern region.

The crucial and still unanswered question is whether these new discoveries in the east can be brought to the surface quickly enough to replace the suspected total decline in output in the traditional fields in the west. Also unanswered is whether the ratio of explored reserves to current output has moved up or down. On neither of these two central questions can we be entirely certain. What we can be certain about is that there are a great many unexplored but geologically promising areas in the Soviet Union, including large areas offshore in the Caspian, Black and Baltic Seas where Soviet naval strength is already heavily deployed. In the event of the Soviet government's giving it sufficient priority there can be very little doubt that the indigenous oil could be found and extracted — given a reasonable period to do so.

The Siberian Policy

In spite of the generally favourable long-term position that the Soviet Union finds itself in in respect of total reserves, it nevertheless faces major obstacles to the rapid exploitation of those reserves. The greatest single obstacle to Soviet energy development is that while most of the coal, oil, gas and hydro-electric power resources lie in the remote regions of Siberia and Central Asia, the chief centres of demand exist in the western part of the country. With distances of up to four thousand miles involved, this has meant that transport is a very important production cost, for not only does the centre obtain most of its natural gas from Central Asia, but much of its coal and oil is transported by rail from the east.

To counter this problem, what is loosely known as the Siberian policy was developed. This involves concentrating industrial investment in the fuel areas and encouraging a movement of labour from the west and central areas into the underpopulated eastern region. This has certainly been assiduously promoted at the highest planning levels and has resulted in a net migration gain to the east. However, it is doubtful whether it is as significant in demographic terms as Soviet demographers claim, as reported earlier in this chapter. Certainly there has been considerable resistance to such a population shift. Despite the financial incentives described earlier it has been difficult to attract, let alone retain, settlers in areas which not only lack the amenities that go with a mature infrastructure but are also extremely inhospitable climatically. Proof of this lies in the prolonged under-utilisation of some of the Siberian hydro dams. Overall the Siberian policy has not proved markedly successful.

Latterly, though not yet publicly acknowledged, the Siberian policy has come under increasing review with a growing feeling that energy and raw material resources will have to be transported from the east to European Russia. One of the principal pressures behind the drastic modification of the Siberian policy comes from the oil and gas ministries, whose demand for increased output simply cannot wait for the more broadly based economic development that the original Siberian policy requires. Instead they are increasingly pursuing a capital-intensive, lightly-manned development strategy giving minimum attention to the development of the general infrastructure. This means in practice the deployment of high technology such as automation, operating from bases outside the region, and the increasing use of helicopters.

There is another major reason, much less discussed let alone publicised, which has conceivably inhibited the fufilment of the official Soviet policy to bring forward the Siberian region on a broad economic front. While Central Asia is markedly underpopulated, its indigenous population is among the fastest growing in the Soviet Union. In the light of the comparative failure of Moscow's policy to attract settlers from the western republics, it is conceivable that the Russians may not wish to develop such non-Russian areas into too economically self-sufficient regions against the possibility that they will chafe at being controlled and directed from such a vast distance in the west.

Finally, a brake not simply on a so-called Siberian policy but on energy development in Siberia by any means, there are very severe technical handicaps. These handicaps include the lack of supporting infrastructure as well as adverse climatic conditions which means that exploration, drilling and pipeline construction can only be undertaken in the winter time. That the extraction of oil and gas from the Siberian fields may be more costly than the Russians are prepared to admit can be seen in the significant expansion of nuclear power generating capacity in the Soviet Ninth Five Year Plan; on the other hand it may be merely a modest attempt at diversification. In 1970 the Soviet Union produced only 3.5 billion kilowatts from such nuclear plants (around 0.5 per cent of total energy output), but in the Ninth Five Year Plan nuclear capacity accounts for 11 per cent of new plants.

The speed at which the Siberian oil and gas fields will be developed is not at all certain, both for technical reasons and for broader political ones — that is, the priority that oil technology imports will be given over, for instance, grain imports whose quantity, despite the U.S.–Soviet agreements, is likely to fluctuate from year to year according to the quality of both the American and Russian harvests. The technical problems alone offer infinite possibilities for bottlenecks. Since we are not primarily concerned with the technical aspects of energy extraction we can only allude to their nature and scope very briefly. The extraction of Siberian gas, for instance, requires the development of an essentially new technology including compressor stations and the drilling of wells of extra large diameter as well as several horizons in a given well at once; also the construction of very large diameter pipelines (1.42 metre pipe, for instance) to lower the cost of piping gas such great distances. Siberian oil also requires a refined technology to transport it from the West Siberian fields to European regions of the Soviet Union, with increasingly larger pumping units to speed the oil on its transcontinental journey. Such technical problems are bound to provide constraints on the fufilment of Soviet energy supply throughout the 1970s.

The first two years of the Soviet Ninth Five Year Plan provides concrete evidence of the underfufilment of energy supply targets because of technical deficiencies. Both the projections for the first five years (1971—5) and those extending to 1980 were admittedly highly ambiguous, designed particularly in the 1975—80 period to provide an energy surplus for export. According to the original Ninth Five Year Plan, oil and gas were to raise their stake in total energy output from 60 to 67 per cent, while coal was to fall back to a lower percentage of total output. Beginning in 1972 there have been serious shortfalls in energy output right up until 1975. Since the predictions for 1975 to 1980 were predicated on the comple-tion of the earlier targets, they must now be seriously in question. Where the Plan envisaged in the period 1975 to 1980 a major shift away from exploration to production drilling, this may now be very much in doubt — that is, unless reserves are allowed to run down. Certainly targets for the 1971—5 period, where rig productivity was expected to rise by 70 per cent in exploratory drilling and 50 per cent in development drilling, can at this stage be discounted. While the growth of coal production has generally exceeded its target throughout the Ninth Five Year Plan, there has been a serious shortfall in oil and gas production up until 1975. The danger for the latter part of the 1970s is that accessible reserves may not keep pace with demand.

Soviet Domestic Energy Demand

Soviet domestic energy requirements have been notoriously difficult to forecast other than by projecting trends from the recent past and attempting to anticipate some of the more obvious changes that may occur and could conceivably influence future demand. Looking at the recent past, there is the surprising fact that over the twenty years from 1950 to 1970 there has been an actual decline in the rate of growth of domestic fuel consumption. Thus from 1950 to 1960 the average annual growth rate was 7.7 per cent, but it was only 6.1 per cent from 1960 to 1965 and a mere 5.3 per cent in 1965–70. The causes for this surprising decline in the rate of growth of energy demand are extremely varied and interesting for the light they shed upon the behaviour of the Soviet economy in general. Unless examined in detail such figures can be quite misleading. On the side favouring an increase in energy demand was the growth in energy-intensive technologies, while among the factors slowing the increase in demand was the decline in the rate of growth of GNP. But probably the most important conditioning factor favouring lower energy consumption was a shift in the Soviet economy from non-efficient to fuel-saving processes. These included the replacement of firewood in domestic use by coal, the switch from steam to diesel and electric traction on the railroads, and the improvement in electric power generation. To this extent the recent past, judged by the figures for the two decades from 1950 to 1970, is not a very appropriate indicator for the future, not least because the switch to more efficient fuels has more or less been accomplished. There is in fact some evidence that the forces likely to push up demand have asserted a definite ascendancy. These arise from a general increase in consumer demand (notably household appliances and cars) and even more from the introduction of energy-intensive processes as an aspect of the Soviet Union's drive towards greater technological efficiency. Meanwhile Soviet energy consumption *per capita* is still about half that of the United States. As the Russians raise the share of oil and gas in their total energy supply this gap will surely close.

So far in examining Soviet energy demand we have confined our examination to domestic demand. But since the Soviet Union has for some time been a net supplier of energy resources to the world market it is also necessary to examine its energy export pattern, past, present and future. Not only is the pattern of direct interest to the major energy-importing countries but it is also of general interest by virtue of providing a clue to Soviet economic policy and particularly foreign economic policy.

Soviet Energy Export Policy

It was during the 1950s that the Soviet Union switched from being a net importer of energy to a net exporter. By 1960 its net export of energy was about 7 per cent of primary energy production. Throughout most of the 1960s the proportion remained at about 12 per cent. The Ninth Five Year Plan for 1971—5 predicted the growth of primary energy production at 6 per cent. Assuming that domestic demand grew at the rate of 5.3 per cent annually (as it did during 1965—70) it would have provided an increment available for export of about 150 million tons of fuel annually. In fact primary energy production grew more slowly than predicted, while domestic demand grew more rapidly, so that by 1975 Soviet energy exports were substantially less than 150 million tons. Most of these exports were accounted for by oil exports of 100 million tons, of which nearly half was sold to Western countries. But by far the greatest quantity of Soviet gas, oil and electric energy exported was delivered to the East European countries which, with the exception of Romania, were seriously deficient in energy. Of all Soviet energy exports in 1970, around one third were exported to the East European Six which, unlike the Soviet Union, depended heavily (about 80 per cent) on solid fuel. If anything this energy dependence has grown in the 1970s.

This brings us to a crucial ambivalence in Soviet energy policy. On the one hand the Soviet Government has repeatedly expressed itself as unwilling to meet the energy import requirements of the East European Six indefinitely; on the other it seems in practice to have unofficially so committed itself. While in the mid-1960s, when the prospects for Soviet oil production and export were unfavourable, there was some Soviet pressure on the East European countries to procure their oil supplies in the Middle East, that phase has now ended. In retrospect it can now be seen that the Soviet Communist Party directives of 1969 authorising a major push to discover and exploit energy resources in Western Siberia were not unconnected with maintaining the energy self-sufficiency of not merely the Soviet Union but also the Soviet bloc as a whole against just such an eventuality as occurred in the Middle East in late 1973. To ameliorate their energy dependence on the Soviet Union there have been extensive plans put forward to boost nuclear power production in the satellite states, but these are very long-term measures and may not relieve the responsibility on the Soviet energy suppliers until the mid-1980s or even 1990.

While the Soviet Union has followed a long-standing policy of tying the economies of its satellite states to its own by vital economic links – Comecon was effectively one of the earliest of postwar preferential trading blocs – there are some noticeable economic disadvantages to both the Soviet Union and its partners in such arrangements. While as sellers they can sometimes demand higher prices than if they were bargaining in a larger market, equally and possibly more frequently they must accept poorer deals than if they were free to negotiate deals without limitation worldwide. What each country gains in having few competitors for its exports, it also loses in having to buy its imports from a narrow range of countries and ultimately goods. These are the general principles which plague Comecon. In energy both the Russians and the East Europeans are losers in the strict economic sense. The Russians receive payment for their energy worth less to them than the goods they could obtain by selling their energy elsewhere; the East Europeans for their part are obliged to buy from a single high-cost energy source with no possibility of buying cheaper energy on the world market. These built-in economic handicaps arising from a closed economic system become less serious when energy cartels like OPEC begin to flex their muscles.

Economic vs Security Interest

The Soviet Union has for some considerable time had a major incentive to sell energy to Western countries in order to obtain hard currencies with which to buy high-technology goods. This has meant that the Soviet government has been prepared to extract indigenous oil often at a cost of up to 15 roubles and more per ton. It has also meant that the Soviet Union has at times been prepared to divert oil from Eastern Europe, where it could have obtained a return of the order of $20 per ton, to sell it to the West at a price of around $10 per ton. The ideological, economic and historical links existing between the Soviet Union and its satellites in Eastern Europe suggest that this policy could not have been casually adopted. It arose in general terms because the high-technology Western goods purchased with Soviet oil exports not only have a high productivity value but also act as prototypes, thereby stimulating industrial innovation. More particularly the Soviet government needs Western technology preeminently in the oil and gas industries for such items as submersible pumps and lighter oil rigs.

Thus economically speaking the Soviet Union has every reason to expand energy exports, by any means. The economic restraints on pursuing an expansionist oil export policy consist then mainly of three elements: the cost of forgoing a high-price guaranteed market in Eastern Europe, the high initial capital cost of extracting Siberian energy, and the potential cost of diverting Soviet domestic energy consumption to allow energy exports to expand. Each of these constraints is surmountable given the gains from selling energy to Western Europe, the United States and Japan, although if Soviet grain harvests continue to produce such poor yields, the extent to which the Soviet industrial economy can avail itself of Western technology will be strictly circumscribed. In the light of the apparent convincing economic rationale for expanding energy exports, the question remains: why does the Soviet Union commit so large a share of its energy exports for the East European states? The short answer is that the Soviet Union wishes to retain her East European satellites on as tight a rein as is possible in an atmosphere of détente for quite traditional reasons of national security. The political advantage to the Soviet Union of supplying such a key commodity is one of the surest guarantees of their remaining virtual client states. There are nonetheless policy options that the Soviet Union has entertained in the past, and may well entertain in the future, that would involve a major break with this basically self-sufficient approach to energy which remains inviolate in spite of the growth of commercial contacts globally.

While the Soviet Union clearly has fairly ample reserves of most primary energy resources, many of them are very costly to extract. Before the Yom Kippur war the possibility of importing increasing supplies of low-cost oil and gas from the Middle East was a very tempting option. While as the OPEC price now stands Middle East oil has lost some of its commercial attractiveness, the possibility of barter deals between the Soviet Union and particular Middle East countries remains a live option. The point should not be overlooked that OPEC represents a cartel, not a single monopoly. Should any member of OPEC, more especially a Middle Eastern member, choose to offer the Soviet Union a barter deal of oil below the OPEC monopoly price in return for Soviet manufactured goods, it is technically free to do so at any time.

The trouble is that from the Soviet Union's point of view she cannot do without Western technology and thus cannot afford to offend the Western industrial nations by perpetuating the OPEC monopoly. Thus at this stage the Soviet Union seems most likely to pursue a policy of stepping up her own energy production with the aid of Western technology and finance, and then to export as much as possible to Western Europe, the United States and especially Japan. The alternative policy for the Soviet Union in the Middle East is not a reassuring one, but although it seems at the moment improbable there is no reason why it should not be scrutinised.

In essence it is a policy of political and diplomatic, even military, expansion in some oil-producing region of the Middle East, sufficiently strongly sustained to allow the Soviet Union to meet not only its own energy requirements but those of Eastern Europe as well. With oil available for domestic and satellite consumption at a marginal cost of production, the Soviet Union would then be free to export its relatively high-cost domestic oil to the West (i.e. on the world market, whose prices she would have already bolstered by drawing off significant supplies of OPEC energy). Such a Soviet energy policy is improbable but not impossible.

Conclusion

In its pursuit of the twin goals of self-sufficiency and diversity of supply, Soviet energy policy has common features with the energy policy of the other superstates, especially the United States, the European Economic Community and China. Like China, which is already self-sufficient in energy, and potentially the United States, the Soviet Union is rich in reserves of the major primary sources of energy. The great weakness of the Soviet position is that a major proportion of these reserves are highly inaccessible and consequently very costly and time-consuming to extract and transport to the centres of population and mature industrialisation. While most of the indications discussed in this chapter would point to an overall Soviet strategy of developing its own indigenous sources of energy, almost certainly with the aid of substantial Western technological assistance and credit financing, there remains the outside possiblity that the Soviet Union may seek to secure its energy self-sufficiency by closer economic links with the Middle East oil-producing states (not unlike the European Economic Community).

To summarily recapitulate the Soviet position on oil reserves — petroleum and natural gas being the most politicised of energy sources since they represent such a high proportion of world trade in energy — it can be said that the immediate problem for the Soviet Union is that the prolific oilfields of the Urals–Volga region which contributed so significantly to Soviet industrial expansion during the 1950s and 1960s are becoming seriously depleted. The anticipated increase in oil production during the 1970s will be derived largely from the West Siberian and western Kazakhstan oilfields lying to the east of the Ural Mountains. Even Western geologists estimate proved and probable reserves of oil in these regions to be about 40 billion barrels (5.5 billion tons), which is roughly equal to the oil estimated to lie beneath the North Slope of Alaska, the richest North American oilfield still to be fully exploited. In the case of natural gas, the Soviet Union is indisputably the best endowed nation in the world, with reserves of 18 trillion cubic metres compared with the next richest, the United States with around 8 trillion cubic metres. Yet more than half Soviet gas reserves lie in permafrost areas, demanding a new technology in both drilling and pipeline laying that has been far from fully mastered, with consequent perennial delays

Although the physical and technical difficulties needing to be overcome in order to exploit the vastly impressive Soviet reserves could hardly be overestimated — both the environment and the climate of Siberia, for instance, are notably hostile, not to say remote — there is also much evidence of poor planning and a lag in technology which has meant the repeated failure of the Soviet Union to reach its energy production targets as laid down in the Five Year Plans. These shortcomings are tacitly acknowledged in the import of Western oil technology and methods in the mid-1970s. Another aspect in which the Soviet petroleum industry is seriously handicapped is its relatively obsolete transport system, chiefly a shortage of adequate pipelines. Almost 40 per cent of oil transported in the Soviet Union is still carried by rail at a cost almost three times that of pipeline transport. In an attempt to improve the coordination of the energy extraction industry in the Soviet Union, a new Ministry of Construction of Enterprises of the Oil and Gas Industry was formed in 1972. It quickly gave priority to pipeline construction and by the mid-1970s, as we described earlier in this chapter, a major pipeline linking the Siberian oilfields with refineries in the Urals was completed, as well as an expanded Friendship Pipeline to Eastern Europe.

Oil

As we have seen earlier in this chapter, the Soviet Union is broadly self-sufficient in oil. This does not mean that local shortages never occur, but they are most often due to transport factors such as a lack of oil pipelines and an overdependence on rail transport which tends to be overextended during the late summer harvest season. Meanwhile the Soviet economy has become accustomed to rely on the foreign exchange earnings that oil exports have provided since the mid-1950s. Until 1969 the largest share of such exports went to non-Communist countries, but in the 1970s more than half of Soviet oil exports have been sent to Eastern Europe, which (exclusive of Romania) relies upon the Soviet Union for more than 80 per cent of its total oil supplies. While, as we have seen, the Soviet Union itself is not likely to make any immediate major purchases of Middle East oil, the possibility of the East European states' seeking increasing quantities of Middle East oil to supplement their chief source of supply is much greater. They have already signed agreements with Iran and Iraq to import supplementary stocks of oil in exchange for manufactured goods and certain technical services. The Soviet Union meanwhile has been encouraging both U.S. and Japanese companies to invest around one billion U.S. dollars to build a 4200 mile pipeline to carry West Siberian oil to the Soviet Far East and Japan, and also carry out the exploitation of offshore oil around Sakhalin.

Gas

By 1975 the Soviet Union was exporting natural gas totalling 8
billion cubic meters to West Germany, France, Italy and
Finland as well as the East European countries. For the future
the richest prospects are the proposals that U.S. companies
develop pipeline, liquefaction and port facilities to permit the
shipment of 20 billion cubic metres of gas annually until
beyond the year 2000 from the Urengov field in Western Siberia
to the U.S. east coast. As described earlier in the chapter the
Urengov field is quite the richest gas deposit in the world, with
reserves of 4–6 trillion cubic metres. If such a mammoth
project were to go ahead it would represent among the most
significant economic elements in the détente between the
superpowers, the more remarkable in that energy is implicitly a
subject of supreme strategic importance.

   A striking element in the shape of future Soviet energy policy
is that despite her immense reserves the Soviet Union quite
clearly needs the technical aid and financial assistance of each
of the three Western superstates, the United States, the
European Economic Community and Japan. The very fact, as
we shall examine in detail in the fifth chapter, that Japan is
almost totally lacking in primary energy resources and yet
possesses among the most advanced technologies in the world
may hold the key to the future development of Siberian energy
and thus determine the direction of Soviet energy policy in the
next decade.

4 China

Unlike each of the three major economic powers we have so far examined — the United States, the European Economic Community and the Soviet Union — which are to varying degrees conservatively predisposed, having existed as entities for periods ranging from two hundred to sixty years (and in the case of the EEC, with national components tracing their origins even more distantly), China is a genuinely and systematically self-conscious revolutionary nation. Though the Soviet Union is impelled by Marxist–Leninist doctrines it has with the passage of time revealed characteristics common to most major industrial nations with an essentially European cultural and philosophical inheritance. This common heritage is manifest in many of the similarities between the three 'European' superstates' approaches to energy policy and the industrialism which it sustains. By contrast China is distinctively non-European and revolutionary in its foreign policy to the extent that it wishes the whole world to comprehend the new Chinese society and ultimately to experience a comparable revolution as part of an 'inevitable historical process'. The Chinese leadership sees its example having its greatest appeal in the non-industrialised countries of Asia, Africa and Latin America.

Thus China's aim is to encourage the 'countryside', the less developed countries, to stand up and challenge the developed 'cities' of the world, first by adopting the Chinese revolutionary experience of overthrowing the traditional regimes with their historic ties with outside colonialist countries, and second by following the example of Maoist society. It is therefore of the utmost importance to China that its revolution should succeed not only for the sake of the people of China but for all those who might be persuaded to follow its example. Thus, much more than Soviet society, the Chinese leadership has been anxious to avoid an ossification of its bureaucracy into a traditionalist hierachical structure; to avoid falling into a 'bourgeois materialism' preoccupied with income and status; and above all, to avoid lapsing into individualism and personal ambition. These are the negative aspects that the Maoists most fear; on the positive side the emphasis is on self-reliance by the individual, the community, the commune and the Chinese nation as a whole. It is because the Chinese nation is so large that Maoism has stressed the commune, small enough to rouse their loyalties and yet large enough to be self-sufficient.

Much of the foregoing has special relevance, as we shall see, for the distinctive way in which China's energy policy has developed, and helps to explain the very early swing to self-sufficiency in energy in the early 1960s maintained ever since. Equally significantly it has so shaped the pattern of China's industrial and agricultural development that alone among the contenders for a place among the superstates China has so far maintained a tradition of extremely low energy consumption. Before going on to describe China's energy policy in detail it is worth pointing out one serious flaw in the advance of Maoism in China, as analysed by Professor Wang Gungwu:[1]

> The Chinese have had considerable trouble with the concept of progress, because the Marxist—Leninist concept of progress is thoroughly alien to them. Marxism—Leninism stems from European ideas of the Enlightenment and from a European conception of progress with a long history, which perhaps reaches its most advanced form in the kind of inevitability that Marx and Lenin presented to the world. In this philosophy, progress — through vast and uncontrollable historical forces — is inevitable. All attempts by scholars inside and outside China to discover whether the Chinese tradition had at any time a similar concept of progress have failed. On the contrary, the Chinese have always been completely convinced that biological cycles govern the universe; and biological cycles translated into political terms become cycles of dynasties, of political success and prosperity inevitably followed by decline and fall.

The fact that the idea of progress is clearly non-Chinese and difficult to absorb into a cyclical tradition is something which in the field of energy may prove to be a positive advantage. For unlike the populations of the other superstates the Chinese people have not yet developed expectations of high energy consumption.

Energy's Role in Industrialisation

During the 1950s China embarked upon a programme of industrialisation similar to that of its political and economic sponsor of this period, the Soviet Union. This involved a concentration on heavy industry, notably iron and steel, non-ferrous metals, machine tools, chemicals, and so on, all of which consumed vast quantities of energy. However, there was a deteriorating relationship between China and the Soviet Union which by 1959 prompted a decision by the Chinese Communist Party Central Committee to modify the Soviet-style concentration on heavy industry and devote considerable attention to improving agriculture. Specifically the Central Committee decided upon rural electrification over a ten-year period, which effectively meant that hydro-thermal power was to be given top priority. In most other respects the Communist regimes of the postwar period were bound by a very narrow industrial base — and after 1960 an absence of foreign capital, technology and personnel — to building upon the energy structure they had inherited. Thus the overall economic development structure, within which energy policy constituted an important factor, aimed first at utilising and strengthening existing industrial enterprises in the north-east and coastal provinces, and second at building new ones in north, north-west, central and south-west China.[2]

Preliminary Energy Estimates

In the first decade of Communist rule in China the energy resources of the nation were far from being fully explored, let alone exploited and developed. It was nevertheless apparent in the early 1950s that the four main sources of energy in order of importance were coal, water power, petroleum and natural gas.

Coal Thermo-electric power, which was the principal supplier to Chinese industry, was governed by the supply of coal available. In 1958 China's reserves were estimated at 1 500 000 million tons, of which more than a third existed in a single province, Shansi. Indeed the greater part of the known coal reserves were located in the northern and especially the north-eastern provinces. The Japanese occupation had historically greatly accelerated coal production in the north-east (in 1933, interest on foreign capital in coal mining in China exceeded that of the domestic capital in the industry).

Water power   China is undoubtedly rich in water power. How rich in economic terms is a matter for debate since much of the potential water power, like the Soviet Union's coal and oil in Siberia, lies a great distance from the current major industrial concentrations. In 1958 China's water power potential was assessed at 580 million kilowatts, drawn from a multitude of river systems of which the three biggest accounted for 75 per cent: the Yangtze river system (40 per cent), the Tibetan river system (20 per cent) and the South-West China international river system (17 per cent). The existence of what must arguably be potentially the richest river power system in the world made possible the highly significant decision to give priority to electrification of the rural areas, which in turn helped to reinforce the priority of agriculture and the development of the most decentralised of all the major energy systems so far described. Nevertheless, apart from the varying distances of some of the major sources of hydro-power from the industrial centres, it was the uneven rainfall that is a characteristic of such a vast continental land mass that in practice puts limits upon the theoretical potential of the Chinese river systems.

Petroleum   Prior to the discovery of the Taching oilfield in 1959, China's oilfields were regarded as distinctly meagre in comparison with its enormous population and industrial ambitions. In the pre-Taching era China's oil reserves were estimated at around 5450 million barrels (around 780 million tons). China's domestic oil production was small and transport was extremely costly, distances were vast and there were few pipelines since it was cheaper to import oil from abroad through seaports which were also the chief industrial centres. (See the section on oil later in this chapter.)

Natural Gas   Apart from suburban Shanghai, where a conveniently close gasfield has existed for some time, the major natural gasfields are to be found in Kansu, Sinkiang, Kwangtung, Fukien, Chekiang and Kiangsu.

Atomic Energy   Although the Soviet Union introduced atomic energy production into China in 1955, it was developed very slowly and was not expanded until at least a decade later. The full extent of China's development of atomic energy for peaceful purposes is not known.

Summary of Energy Dispositions, 1949–60

Reserves in 1960 were put at 9.6 trillion tons of coal and 5.9 billion tons of oil which, even if it were an overestimate, would be sufficient to support the expansion of Chinese industrial growth in the next few decades. This could be the more readily achieved since a very high proportion of energy consumption in China is still devoted to the creation of electricity for heavy industry. Thus in 1960 China's heavy industry sector absorbed 90 per cent of total consumption (this compares with 75 per cent in the Soviet Union and 50 per cent in the United States); in fact in 1960 only 5 per cent of China's domestic supply was consumed by households (compared with 30 per cent in the United States). These are interesting by-products of differing economic creeds and the priorities that stem from them. Arising from the energy sources just described it can be seen that in 1960 the Chinese economy was run almost entirely on coal, with coal accounting for 54 per cent of energy consumed. Hydro-power provided 26 per cent of energy consumed, and petroleum a mere 3 per cent. It is interesting to note that this energy distribution corresponds roughly to the United States in 1900, when 88 per cent of its energy was derived from coal, 5 per cent from petroleum and 3 per cent from natural gas and hydro-power.

The political goal of self-sufficiency in energy (and to some extent raw materials) which, as we have seen, has become an increasingly common aspect of the other superstates has been the goal of China's leadership since 1960, when Soviet assistance was abruptly and dramatically withdrawn.[3] Nowhere are the sometimes heroic efforts of the Chinese leadership to achieve self-sufficiency more clearly demonstrated than in the post-1949 development of the petroleum industry in China. Where prior to 1949 more than 90 per cent of China's oil was imported, by 1973 Chinese crude oil production had reached a total of 50 million metric tons, making China the fourteenth largest oil producer in the world and an oil exporter. While Chinese industrial and economic data available are far from complete, not least because energy is a defence question, it is helpful to trace the evolution of China's oil industry and the interaction between political goals and the technological demands of industrial development.

The Years of Foreign Aid

Immediately after the assumption of power by the Communist government in 1949, exploration and production of crude oil was noticeably accelerated. It was not, however, until the beginning of the First Five Year Plan (1953—7) that China began to receive technical assistance and material aid from the Soviet Union on a scale to suggest that an indigenous oil-producing industry was contemplated. At this stage most of the investment and effort were expended on exploration, although four new refineries with shale oil distillation factories were reconstructed and expanded. The Langchow refinery was probably the most advanced in the Soviet bloc at this time. From the Soviet Union itself, as from Czechoslovakia, Hungary, Poland, East Germany and Romania, came the skills and experience which China lacked to establish her own petroleum industry.

The next phase was the Second Five Year Plan (1958—62) which was to fall into two quite different parts: that period lasting from 1958 to 1960 when the Chinese nation was engaged in the Great Leap Forward campaign, and the years 1960—1 when a period of stagnation in the petroleum industry was experienced. The Great Leap Forward, which was an economic spurt embracing much more than the energy sector, set itself a target of 5—6 million tons and the completion of a pipeline between Karamai oilfield and Tushantsu refinery as well as a railway between Hami and the Langchow refinery; all these aims were fulfilled, thereby strengthening the links between Central Asia and coastal China. Nevertheless, whatever progress was made in the establishing of an indigenous oil-producing industry, the underlying fact was that throughout the 1950s China's industrial development was sustained by Soviet oil imports, which reached a total of 3 million tons in 1959. Altogether, that is from 1950 to 1968, China imported around 24 million tons of

Soviet crude oil worth about 1 billion U.S. dollars. Then in 1960 the Sino-Soviet split, which had been impending for some time, suddenly took place. Soviet aid ceased immediately and Soviet plans for the expansion of the oil industry were simply withdrawn. Less abruptly, but no less surely, the arrival of equipment from Eastern Europe slowed down and eventually ceased.

Meanwhile, as part of the Great Leap Forward, the policy of Walking on Two Legs was developed with the aim of creating a countrywide network of initially small industrial and other enterprises (such as mining) based on local resources and manpower while larger state-funded enterprises continued to be set up by the state construction corporations. It was seen as a way of making a breakthrough on the construction front and establishing industry away from the coast in rural areas. During this period hundreds of small wells were opened, most of which were to prove uneconomic and subsequently had to be closed. Nevertheless, there were some significant producers that developed from these small beginnings, about all that could reasonably be expected from such a pattern not notably suited to a commodity like petroleum which needs to be drilled, transported and marketed in bulk.

Period of Self-Reliance

There can be little doubt that the most important date in the postwar development of China's petroleum industry was 1959, when the Taching oilfield was first discovered in the north-east. A very large oilfield, it combined the advantages of lying close to the major industrial centres and the industry's main market. A crash programme to develop the new field was put in hand immediately. The Sino-Soviet breach of the following year only served to accelerate its development and underline its significance in China's future industrial growth.[4] For although Chinese oil production had reached 6 million tons, China still needed to import oil to meet the shortfall between expanding production and an even faster expanding industry. Since the Soviet Union had been China's principal external supplier, providing an amount equal to half China's domestic production in 1959, Taching offered the challenge of demonstrating China's self-sufficiency and especially her lack of dependence on the Soviet

Union. Clearly such an aim could not be achieved instant-
aneously but that it needed to be achieved and achieved rapidly
was among the most overriding political imperatives facing the
Chinese leadership in the early 1960s. Before long Taching's
significance greatly transcended energy policy, and it quickly
became a model for China's new policy of national self-reliance.

Imports of crude oil ceased in 1961, though refined oil
imports continued to come in right up until 1969. Nevertheless,
it is probably true to say that by 1963 China had made itself
largely self-sufficient in oil. Gradually the export of crude oil
became a real possibility as the Chinese switched their efforts,
hitherto highly dispersed, to the exploitation of Taching and
rapid development of the oilfields in the Eastern provinces.

Before long Taching was producing 30 million tons annually,
or about five times China's total production in 1959, leaving
about one third of production available for export with reputed
reserves of 900 million tons. In 1962 the Shengli oilfield in
north Shantung was explored and by 1964 it had already
commenced production, while in 1964 the Takang oilfield was
earmarked for priority development. With substantial reserves
of coal, water and oil, the indigenous energy reserves to fuel a
major industrial advance were now realised to lie to hand, giving
an enormous psychological fillip to the Chinese people. Not
that the appropriation of those reserves was likely to be
straightforward. As with the West European states ringing the
North Sea, the technological challenge was immense with much
of the oil lying offshore. Both Shengli and Takang extend
offshore, for instance, while the major offshore fields recently
discovered include the Gulf of Pohai, the Taiwan Straits (highly
controversial in the light of the political history of the area and
the new ocean bed and offshore limits) and the South China
Sea.

In the wake of the Soviet withdrawal of its oil specialists and
of its planning and exploration papers, productivity inevitably
dropped in both the oilfields and the refineries. Thus, although
there was a deep-seated commitment to energy self-sufficiency
in political terms, in practical terms the shortfall needed to be
made up somehow. In the very early 1960s there were
unsuccessful attempts to import oil from Algeria. Meanwhile
the search for indigenous oil began in earnest. It was the
stepped-up oil exploration programme on the Sungari Liao plain

in 1959 that led overnight to the discovery of the Taching
(Great Joy) oilfield. In turn it was largely due to Taching that
by the mid-1960s Chinese oil production was able to pass the
10 million ton mark; Taching, that is, and the discoveries at
Shengli in Shantung province and Takang in Hapei province.
The next great surge of oil development was to take place
during the Great Cultural Revolution in the late 1960s, which
had the overall effect of greatly increasing energy demand.
There was, besides the need to discover oil, strong evidence to
suggest that China contained great oil reserves. Among these
pieces of evidence was the existence of oilfields on the
boundaries of China, specifically the Sakhalin oilfield in the
north-east, the Siberian fields to the north, and the Burmese
and Assamese fields to the south, which may have proved
sources of future friction if no Chinese oil had been discovered.
Deprived of Soviet materials the Chinese reluctantly turned to
the capitalist countries of Western Europe (the United States
having no commercial and very little diplomatic contact at this
time), chiefly Italy, Germany and Britain, for refining and
petro-chemical plants in the early stages of their self-sufficiency
programme. That it must be judged a success can be seen in the
fulfilment of its announced targets such as the fourth Five Year
Plan (1971—5) which aimed at increasing oil production
threefold, representing a target of 70 million tons for 1975 —
which looks like having been reached comfortably. At 1973 levels
China's known oilfields would last at least until 2000, but if as
seems likely the levels are significantly raised, either more
oilfields will have to be discovered or the switch to other fuels
will have to be intensified, as in most other superstates.

Future Energy Prospects

Reviewing China's overall energy sources it would be easy to be
so taken up with the dramatic discoveries of oil and natural gas
that we overlook the fact that they remain secondary sources,
far behind both coal and water power in importance. The
rapidity of the recent development of China's petroleum
industry makes this easy to appreciate. Though they have
developed far less spectacularly coal and water power remain
the chief energy sources, especially coal. With reserves estimated
at 1 trillion tons China is the third best endowed coal country

in the world, following in importance the Soviet Union with 4.2 trillion tons and the United States with 1.1 trillion tons. Most of this great coal potential is as yet unrealised. In hydro-potential China is among the best endowed nations anywhere, though its chances of being exploited rapidly are reduced by the fact that many of these rivers lie in the thinly populated areas of Yunnan and Tibet. Despite the fact that the average growth rate of China in the early 1970s was around 5 per cent and her industrial growth was double that figure, China has so far been able to keep down the rate of increase of energy demand to a mere 6 per cent. Ally this with the evidence of vast energy reserves, and one must conclude that for the short-term and even medium-term future, China's energy reserves are more significant for the potential foreign earnings they can buy her and the speed at which they can be made available to her energy-hungry industrial neighbour states, notably Japan, Korea, Vietnam, Thailand and the Philippines.

Oil

As we have seen with estimates of energy reserves elsewhere, there is extensive scope for debate about the precise size of energy reserves in most energy-rich countries. China is no exception. Nevertheless there is no dispute about the fact that China's oil reserves and shale oil deposits dwarf all others in Asia (exclusive of the Middle East). According to the Continent-al Oil Corporation, China has known reserves of oil amounting to 2700 million tons, or about 56 per cent of all Asia's known reserves. In addition the same American oil company estimates China has 4000 million tons of as yet undiscovered oil reserves, on the basis of the known geological strata, and so on. This represents an overwhelming 76 per cent of Asia's undiscovered estimated reserves, which remains a highly speculative figure but underlines the rich untapped oil potential lying within China's borders. There are also believed to be 20 000 million tons of shale oil and 30 trillion cubic feet of natural gas lying beneath Chinese soil. Finally, according to the Economic Commission for Asia and the Far East, China could become one of the world's largest producers of offshore oil, helped by the shallow nature of her coastal waters, especially the Gulf of Pohai and Taiwan Straits oilfields.

With an obvious oil surplus in view if China were to maintain more or less her current pattern of consumption, it is useful to project the nature of China's export pattern not only for what it may herald about the nature of China's external relations but also for the effect it is likely to have on the direction of her domestic economy in the late 1970s. In 1973, for instance, when China began her first noticeable build-up of oil exports, she exported around 2.5 million tons: 1 million tons to Japan, 800 000 tons to North Korea, 500 000 tons to North Vietnam and 100 000 to Hong Kong. By the following year, with the rise in Middle East oil prices, her oil exports jumped dramatically to around 6.5 million tons: 4 million tons to Japan, 1 million to North Korea, 500 000 to North Vietnam, 300 000 to Hong Kong, 200 000 to the Philippines and 125 000 tons to Thailand. By 1975, China's oil exports were estimated to have reached about 10 million tons: 8 million tons to Japan, 1 million tons to North Korea, and 500 000 tons to North Vietnam, greatly enhancing China's bargaining position with Japan and under-lining the powerful links between China and the Communist states within her generally acknowledged sphere of influence in the shape of North Korea and now Vietnam. By 1980 China expects to export an absolute minimum of 20 million tons of petroleum.

Even by 1974 China had reached the point of becoming the world's fourteenth largest oil producer, with an annual pro-duction of 50 million tons. The Chinese Government are already anticipating doubling this production figure within two to three years. Much of this dramatic expansion will take place at Taching, which currently produces 40 per cent of China's total oil. More remarkable even than the growth in domestic production is the continued restraint exercised in domestic demand.

With a population of 800 million people and a relatively advanced economy by the standards of much of Asia, China consumes only 50 kilos *per capita* per year, which is not much different from consumption *per capita* in India with a far lower material standard of living. Oil represents only about one fifth of all energy consumed in China, underlining China's achievement of energy diversity of supply *and* self-sufficiency, goals which most of the other superstates are still striving to achieve at some future date in the 1980s. In the case of oil, besides the obvious fact of China's history of low energy consumption and generally low energy consumption expectations for the future, energy demand has been effectively restrained by high prices.[5]

Conclusion

An important element in China's Cultural Revolution was the debate about the use of modern technology. The subsequent adoption of a markedly more 'open door' policy in the industrial field than hitherto ushered in a new willingness to adopt Western technology where it seemed appropriate. A major question that will become more pressing in the late 1970s is: can China's oil exports be deployed to pay for this import of Western technology?

China's potential demand, currently restrained by custom, by high prices for domestic consumption and by a shortage of refining capacity, could explode if the appropriate decisions to exploit the oil reserves rapidly and purchase foreign technology with the proceeds were to lead to Western-style industrialisation. If current plans to produce 100 million tons by 1977, setting aside 20 million tons for export, are carried through, it could be the first step in the escalation of energy demand in China which in the period 1975–82 could bring in $30 billion worth of foreign earnings. But to obtain such an influx of foreign income would require massive investment in refining, transport and storage. The immediate question therefore, is how far should China rely on Western technology and finance, or will China continue to pursue a policy of national self-reliance?

5 Japan

More than any of the other four superstates, Japan represents the supreme example of a major industrial economy whose outstanding postwar growth rate has been based on an accelerating rate of energy consumption by the industrial sector. Throughout most of the 1960s and right up until 1972, Japan's annual rate of increase was around 12 per cent. Despite this spectacular growth performance, Japan's *per capita* energy consumption is only about one third of that of the United States. But unlike the United States, Japan has extremely meagre natural resources. The year 1974 brought home to the Japanese people as never before just how lacking in raw materials the Japanese archipelago was together with the existence of a considerable current demand to import raw materials to sustain the material standards of her heavily populated islands. In principle none of this was particularly new, only more acute than ever before.

Ever since the Meiji period the development of the Japanese economy has been founded on foreign trade because of the lack of material resources and the abundance of human resources. In consequence, in 1972 Japan accounted for around 14 per cent of total world trade, and since her export trade was worth $28.6 billion compared with $23.5 billion worth of imports, she boasted a trade surplus of more than $5 billion. Significantly, around 80 per cent of Japan's export manufactures were from heavy industrial goods and chemical products, making her just that much more vulnerable when energy imports either dried up or became prohibitively expensive. The year of reckoning came of course in 1973, and even more acutely in terms of its consequences in 1974.

The stark character of Japan's energy larder is not always fully appreciated outside that country. Petroleum deposits in Japan account for a mere 0.005 per cent of world reserves, coal a tiny 0.3 per cent, while hydroelectric power which once used to account for a major proportion of electric power generation (of which Japan produces the third greatest quantity in the world) has since the early 1960s slipped back until it is now exceeded by thermal power generation. This has meant that as Japan's industrial economy grew by leaps and bounds in the postwar period, and particularly during the 1960s, her energy consumption, largely imported, has rocketed. Thus total energy consumption grew around threefold between 1962 and 1972, with petroleum consumption showing a fivefold increase over the same period, coal and electric energy growing by a factor of 1.4, and natural gas fivefold. All this time the distribution of energy resources demanded by the Japanese economy was making it more and more vulnerable year by year as it switched from coal to petroleum. Thus in 1962 coal accounted for 36 per cent of energy consumption and petroleum 46 per cent; but by 1972 coal had fallen to 17 per cent while petroleum had soared to 75 per cent. This meant that Japan was becoming dangerously exposed to external economic pressures, for not only did her total imported energy supplies rise from 52 per cent in 1962 to 86 per cent in 1972, but almost all her energy imports were derived from a single region, namely the Middle East. Among the superstates, only the European Economic Community was even remotely comparable to Japan in its vulnerability to the determined application of a raw material producers' cartel in the shape of OPEC which was to bring the Japanese economic miracle to an end with brutal abruptness.

Political Posture

The year of the Yom Kippur war in the Middle East and the consequent OPEC oil embargo was also a seminal date in the postwar history of Asia in that it saw the conclusion of a political settlement to the perennial war in Indochina. Unlike the earlier settlement of 1954, which provided a framework that might have lasted for a number of years, the 1973 settlement was patently a means of securing an American withdrawal with a minimum loss of face and left unclear the precise set of national alignments in the Indochinese peninsular. Indeed, as Professor A. M. Halpern points out,[1] the 1973 Indochina accords were preceded by profound changes in the foreign policies of the major powers. These changes were widely understood by the powers concerned – the United States, the

Soviet Union and China — as creating the basis and the general
climate for the more particularist and regional accords which
followed.

Both as a regional power, the only advanced industrial Asian
country, and as an extra-regional world economic power or
superstate, Japan's position in Asia was fundamentally affected.
Despite the importance of the accord for Japan, the changes in
Japan's foreign policy have been gradual rather than spectacular. They have included a general expansion of Japan's
diplomatic and commercial relations with China and North
Korea without any noticeable rupture in her relations with
either Taiwan or South Korea. While the importance of the
United States–Japan Security Treaty inhibited her from taking
any positive action likely to breach that treaty, the Japanese
people have long felt a deep revulsion towards American
involvement in Vietnam. The 1973 settlements, while they were
seen as a formal cover for a more or less dignified American
withdrawal, were not only enthusiastically welcomed but
positively enhanced U.S.–Japanese relations. These political
considerations far outweighed any loss in American commercial
purchases of Japanese supplies to prosecute the Vietnam
struggle.

Japan's role in the south-east Asian region is psychologically
a mixture of being profoundly aware of her interdependence
but deeply anxious to maintain a low political profile. Thus
Japan is quite the most preeminent regional economic power
— her trade with the area amounted to more than $10 billion in
1972 — but in political terms she is more likely to respond to
events than to create them. While Japan tends to dominate the
market in South Korea, Taiwan and Thailand, she is herself
heavily dependent on raw material imports from both Australia
and Indonesia, worth $2.2 billion and $1.2 billion respectively
in 1972. It is the extent of Japanese economic investment,
while for the most part clearly beneficial to the host countries,
that has stimulated most of the residual anti-Japanese feeling in
the south-east Asian region, a factor which the Japanese
Government has been at great pains to identify and remedy.
Since Japan's day-to-day economic relations are conducted in
practice almost entirely by her businessmen, her political goals
are sometimes subordinated to her more immediate economic
advantage.

There is undoubtedly an unresolved tension in Japan's political posture which has become increasingly apparent since the 1973 energy crisis. On the one hand Japan has so far been content to play a relatively passive political role in the Asian region as well as disowning any ambitions to great power status. On the other hand Japan is not only the predominant Asian economic power but destined to become once again a world power. Third to the United States and the Soviet Union in economic terms, Japan is indubitably a superstate, as her post-1973 resource diplomacy underlines.

Post-1973 Energy Policy

As we have already outlined at the beginning of this chapter, Japan, traditionally lacking in natural resources in general, is especially short of energy and almost totally without any indigenous sources of petroleum. When the OPEC nations imposed their unprecedented price increases in 1973, the Japanese economy suffered the most comprehensive setback it had received in the entire postwar period, more damaging in its immediate effects than that experienced by any of the other superstates. The response of the Japanese Government, while clearly shaken by the scale of the challenge thrown down to it, was emphatic and decisive. Its strategy was based on three main priority responses: (1) to economise on oil consumption immediately; (2) to build new enlarged reserves of oil, and (3) to seek out fresh sources of crude oil.

By November 1973 the Japanese government had imposed a 10 per cent cut in consumption of both oil and electric power, passed two major pieces of legislation (one for balancing oil supplies equitably among consumers and the other for stabilising peoples' livelihood) and declared a state of national emergency. These measures, while amply justified and inflicting widespread hardship on the Japanese people, barely slowed the effects of the crisis on the Japanese economy. To illustrate the calamitous effects on Japan's economy, by February 1974 the nation's oil stocks had plummeted to a mere 50 days' supply (by September they had begun to pick up again and reached the comparative safety of 70 days' supply). In an effort to reduce consumption, the government directed the price of oil to be raised at each phase of distribution. By August this had begun to have beneficial effects, and the government price freeze was lifted. The attempt to reduce demand, however, was far from over, as the government announced its intention of cutting consumption in 1975 by a further 10 per cent.

Meanwhile Japan joined the global efforts of the consumer nations to create a common front both to cope with the effects of the quadruple oil price rise and to mount a concerted response to any future moves initiated by OPEC. Arguably the chief of these responses was an entirely new body, the International Energy Agency, which arose from among the ranks of the OECD countries to coordinate a programme of crisis management called forth by the truly daunting scale of the energy problem. Among the major oil-consuming countries represented on the International Energy Agency, Japan was by far the most dependent on oil supplies from the Persian Gulf. In the early 1970s, around 90 per cent of Japan's total oil imports, and therefore effectively the same proportion of her total consumption, was derived from this region. Thus, in spite of her general unwillingness to play a political role commensurate with her economic size and strength, the oil price rise catapulted Japan, however reluctantly, into the most crucial crisis management body in the Western world. For some years Japan had paid tribute to the concept of international interdependence, meanwhile playing a low-key political role as if Japan counted for about the same as Australia in the counsels of the world. By late 1973 she could no longer assume such modest pretensions and in the very process of preserving her vital national interests began to deploy the political and economic power which she had for so long kept in reserve. In the form of the International Energy Agency Japan began to discover that when allied with some combination of other superstates she possessed more political persuasion than she had previously suspected, and this at a moment when she felt acutely vulnerable. It is one of the ironies of contemporary history that Japan, long upheld as the prime example of rapid industrialisation in the postwar period, yet at the same time regarding herself as virtually without political power, should discover her latent political strength at the very moment when her economic growth was effectively checked and her self-doubts about the quality of her industrial society were most persistent. Prior to 1973 Japan's amazing economic growth performance had been based on cheap and

abundant oil. Now abruptly parted from this essential commodity and deeply conscious that commodity cartels could
create a fashion, Japan's prime responsibility in seeking to
preserve the continuity of her industrial economy, however
modified in the future, was to secure a stable supply of natural
resources in general and energy resources in particular. In
examining the means adopted by Japan in pursuing what is
commonly termed resource diplomacy we are able to study in
accentuated form a process which is common to each of the
superstates, that is, the securing of stable supplies of raw
materials.

Energy Recovery Programme

The spearhead of the Japanese Government's energy recovery
programme is the powerful Ministry of International Trade and
Industry (MITI). MITI's programme strategy can be summarised
under six main heads: (1) the active development of oil in
Japan's offshore continental shelf: (2) the direct acquisition of
crude oil from oil-producing states on a government-to-
government basis; (3) the increased stockpiling of oil until by
1979 the nation should possess a 90-day supply in reserve;
(4) the readjustment, mainly slimming down, of Japan's energy
industries; (5) the development of new energy technologies; and
(6) the promotion for the long term of both the nuclear and
solar energy industries. Overall, MITI plans a restructuring of
the entire industrial economy so that the growth in oil
consumption can be slowed to the extent that by 1980
consumption should be kept down to 800 million kilolitres of
crude oil, a very much lower figure than would have been
reached without a reconstruction. The means employed to
achieve these objectives necessarily involved increasing Government intervention. The stockpiling policy, for instance, offers
Government loans on very generous terms to the private oil
companies to enable them to buy or build new storage facilities
and to buy crude oil for stockpiling. The so-called Sunshine
Project, the brainchild of MITI, also involves Government
expenditure in the development of new technologies for using
new sources of energy, such as solar, geothermal, coal gasifi-
cation, and hydrogen energy. MITI's recovery programme
projected that if its measures were fully adopted then by the

close of 1975 the oil recession would have come to an end and
supplies of both energy and raw materials would have at least
stabilised. Broadly speaking its optimism was vindicated by
events.

During 1975 Japan's newly created Advisory Committee on
Energy was heavily engaged in promoting government-to-
government deals in oil (see chapters 3 and 4 on the Soviet
Union and China) and generally diversifying away from the
Middle East which nevertheless remained Japan's principal
regional supplier. At home the Committee was making con-
structive suggestions on the reorganisation of the energy industry
and the overall reconstruction of industry to reduce its rate of
energy consumption. For what is striking about the adaptive-
ness of the Japanese economy is its ability to modify energy
consumption without apparently altering long-term production
goals.

Thus by September 1975, with inflation virtually under
control, the Japanese Prime Minister, Takeo Miki, revoked
the Government's previous tight money policy and announced anti-recession measures which were intended to push
up the country's growth rate of around 1 per cent to
somewhere around 6 per cent in the second half of the fiscal
year. Any immediate return to the growth rates which had
existed before the oil price rises was not feasible, he warned. At
the same time with a favourable price performance the Japanese
Government was free to stimulate demand — including substantial loans to small businesses. For despite the growth of
several major industrial conglomerates Japan's industrial structure is characterised by the parallel existence of large numbers
of unincorporated enterprises. In 1972, for instance, unincorporated enterprises accounted for 73 per cent of total
private establishments, while incorporated enterprises unsurprisingly accounted for only 27 per cent. Even in manufacturing, small establishments with fewer than five employees
accounted for 51 per cent of the total manufacturing establishments, while only 4800 establishments employed more than
300 persons. This particular industrial structure may provide the
clue to why the Japanese economy has proved so responsive to
demand and so resilient in absorbing energy cuts while
maintaining reasonable production levels.

Resource Diplomacy

Because of her combination — albeit not unique — of deficient natural resources and a high industrial output, Japan practises the most highly developed brand of resource diplomacy of any of the superstates. Geographically there are two preeminent target areas for Japan's resource diplomacy. First, there are the oil-rich states of the Middle East, and second, there are the two Communist superstates, the Soviet Union and China. In the case of the former, Japan's general strategy has been no different from that of either the United States or the European Economic Community members, that is, to strengthen all possible economic and technological links and to provide the technical skills and investment which the Middle East countries most require — in return for stable oil supplies. In the case of the Soviet Union and China, the Japanese have already embarked on several vast projects which broadly speaking involve the transfer of Japanese technology in some form or another (together with bank loans) in return for long-term bulk supplies of crude oil. Some of the very largest of these joint projects also potentially involve the United States, underlining both their gigantic scale and the fact that they are politically conceived, classic exercises in fact of resource diplomacy.

Siberian Resources Development

In all there were by 1975 around five major projects to exploit Siberian natural resources in which the Japanese had become politically and financially involved to a greater or lesser degree. Even by 1974 loan agreements had been signed and work already commenced on two of them, the Far East forestry development plan and the south Yakutia coking coal development. Under the protocol covering them both, signed in April 1974, Japan granted the Soviet Union long-term credits up to a limit of $1050 million for the development of coal deposits and natural gas prospecting in Yakutia and the development of timber resources in the Soviet Far East. In the Yakutia part of the agreement Japan agreed to provide an immediate loan of around $450 million to the Soviet Union which in return guaranteed to provide supplies of 14.4 million tons of coal from 1983 to 1998. Taking the two projects together it can be said that the Japanese credit will be used very largely by Soviet organisations to buy Japanese machines, equipment, ships and any materials necessary to carry out the two joint projects. The prime energy benefits for Japan from the two projects are most decidedly the prospect of bringing in coking coal and ultimately natural gas from Siberia instead of from much further afield. The joint agreement, which is for a twenty-year period, provides the Soviet Union with the kind of sophisticated transportation, hoisting and earth-moving equipment, for want of which the Soviet energy programme would otherwise lag behind badly. Under the Soviet–Japanese agreements Yakutian coal exports to Japan are predicted to reach around 5 million tons by 1986. The agreements are undoubtedly mutually advantageous. On the Soviet side the overall development of the coal industry in Eastern Siberia is likey to be speeded up, for not only is the capital now available to import the required equipment but the coking coal will also be made available to Siberian industrial enterprises. On their side the Japanese steel industry have secured the essential prerequisite for steady expansion, a stable supply of coking coal for an extended period.

But if such resource diplomacy is essential to the health of the Japanese economy, it is also likely to become an increasingly important factor in the economies of the hitherto autarchic Soviet and Chinese economic systems. A classic case in point is the Tyumen oil development plan which was shelved in October 1974 as a result of the 'abrogation' of the U.S.–Soviet Commerce Treaty by the U.S. Congress. Just how significant this was for the Soviet economy may be gauged by the fact that the Tyumen project was one of the largest, if not the largest Soviet industrial project in the Soviet Union's Tenth Five Year Plan. Its difficulties graphically illustrate not only the Soviet economy's need for foreign technology but also the hazards of tri-nation commercial agreements on the grand scale.

The Tyumen project comprises three major elements, all of which are thoroughly typical of such projects and may be usefully examined. First – and normally this is the starting point for such agreements – one or a combination of the parties to the agreement must be prepared to put up the financial credit on a very long-term basis, often so long-term that only a government could ever underwrite such credit arrangements.

Thus in the case of Tyumen the Japanese Government (or alternatively Japan and the United States) might provide the Soviet Union with the necessary bank loans. Second, the remaining party (or parties) to the agreement would use such loans to buy equipment and machines from the original signatory nations. Thus the Soviet Union buys machines from Japan (or Japan and the United States) which enable her to carry out the project which, it is presumed, is to their mutual benefit in its end product as well as its financing and purchasing means and methods. Third, in the final aspect of the transaction, which may take some years to come to fruition and for which there must first exist a favourable political climate if any major nation is to forgo the primary benefits for such an extended period, the non-financing party supplies the strategic raw materials upon which so much time has been spent and so much political prestige put at risk. In the Tyumen project the Soviet Union would undertake to provide Japan (or Japan and the United States) with vast quantities of crude oil and natural gas. It is in such intricate political arrangements that resource diplomacy finds its fulfilment, with consequences for the pattern of both political and commercial relations between the superstates which have not yet begun to be fully assessed. In the case of relations between the superstates and the specifically oil-rich Middle East states, where the latter possess the raw materials, especially energy, *and* gigantic financial surpluses accumulating, resource diplomacy assumes a different character again, but one that is best described in a general rather than a specifically Japanese context. The brittle character of some of these tri-nation schemes, most especially in the early stages before any irrevocable commitments have been made, is well illustrated by the collapse of the Tyumen plan — whether temporarily or permanently is uncertain.

Thus, to summarise the course of Japan's resource diplomacy to date, it can be stated unequivocally that in a period when Japan's trade with the industrial countries in general slackened, as did Japan's own domestic economy and that of the majority of the Western industrial countries, the proliferation of commercial deals with the major oil producers and the two superstates of the Communist bloc assumed ever-growing importance. Statistically, since 1973 Japan doubled her exports to the Soviet Union, China and the seven oil-producing countries — Indonesia, Iran, Iraq, Saudi Arabia, Kuwait, Venezuela and Nigeria — as a whole. From an initial position in the early 1970s, when Japan was closely linked with the Western industrial countries, notably the United States, Australia, Canada and the European Economic Community, more or less constantly in that order, Japan has moved progressively toward closer diplomatic and commercial links with the Communist bloc and the OPEC nations. The self-sufficiency in oil of the latter two groups has provided the most effective stimulus to Japanese exports that could have possibly been devised, most spectacularly is this true in the case of the OPEC countries, whose newly boosted purchasing power has proved a magnet for the exporters of the entire industrialised world. This can be best illustrated by the prediction of the U.S. Commerce Department that the Middle East will have become America's largest overseas market by 1980, when at current prices it may be worth something of the order of $10 billion to U.S. exporters. Though the Japanese Government has refrained from making any comparable prediction for Japanese exporters, its private intentions and expectations are not noticeably different from those of the Americans.

Reshaping of the Economy

In coping with the oil price rise it must be remembered that Japan's consumption of all forms of energy and natural resources is second only to that of the United States, and indeed highest in terms of GNP *per capita* consumption. This is not surprising given that Japan's swift economic growth was based on the creation of vast heavy engineering and chemical industries at a time when imported energy was both plentiful and cheap. One of the principal reasons why Japan was content to allow the perpetuation of an industrial structure that acquiesced in having 99 per cent of its oil imported, and ended by gobbling up 20 per cent of the natural resources consumed annually by the non-Communist world, was that Japan had grown to industrial maturity under the shelter of the American umbrella and had forsaken the habit of viewing international commerce in a political framework within which it has habitually operated.

The Petroleum Industry

No sector of the Japanese economy was as devastated financially by the 1973 oil price rises as that of the Japanese petroleum industry. As the unprecedented decline in demand began to deepen, it was not long before it became apparent that the whole structure and capacity of the industry was far too cumbersome for the existing demand. To illustrate the collapse in profits among the largest energy corporations, Nippon Oil, which retained the largest share of the Japanese oil market in 1974 and was second among companies of any sort in terms of gross earnings, was not even included among the top one hundred Japanese companies with the largest profits. Such a falling away in profitability, typical of the industry, called for a drastic restructuring, which is precisely what the Japanese Government was forced to embark upon by the beginning of 1975.

By August 1975, MITI had unveiled its plans to regroup (or group) most Japanese oil firms. This reorganisation is to create three or four major oil groups to carry out all the traditional tasks of the oil industry — resource development, importing, refining and sales — within a much honed-down overall structure. The MITI plan brought together under a simplified organisational structure a total of eighteen oil refining and sales companies and more than fifty petroleum resources development corporations. The chief immediate gains are mostly in the import, stockpiling and transportation sectors, but there is expected to be a general improvement in total performance and a rationalisation of the slimming-down process. Since many of these companies were heavily deficit-ridden, they were mostly only too willing to cooperate closely with the Ministry's attempts to provide a more rationalised structure for the industry. In the longer term MITI wants the Japanese oil market to be divided equally (i.e. 50 per cent each) between Japanese and foreign oil companies. Recently the indigenous firms had been losing ground rapidly to the often much more diversified foreign oil companies. The point had even been reached where the Japanese oil refining industry was operating at only 63 per cent of capacity, the lowest for thirteen years.

The Coal Industry

While petroleum was so readily available and therefore cheap, the coal industry in Japan could hardly be expected to prosper except as a supplier of specialised industrial fuels such as coking coal. In the decade immediately prior to 1973 the Japanese coal industry was in steady decline, a decline which the Japanese Government did very little to arrest as many of the West European governments attempted to do over the same period. The striking character of that decline can be demonstrated in the following figures. In 1963 there were 306 coal mines in Japan, by 1973 there were only 37 coal mines still operating. In 1963 the Japanese coal industry produced 50 million tons, by 1973 output had fallen to 20 million tons. In 1963 the Japanese coal industry employed 135 000 workers, by 1973 the total workforce had dropped to 25 000. Most striking of all, and reflecting the growth in oil consumption as well as the decline of coal as a primary energy source in relative as well as absolute terms, coal fell from providing 24 per cent of Japan's energy demand in 1963 to a minuscule 4.5 per cent in 1973. In the post-1973 situation, Government policy is to provide money for the opening up of new mines at home and the securing of steady supplies from Australia, the Soviet Union, China and the United States. Unfortunately, coal mines once closed are not easily reopened, and neither the domestic Japanese coal industry nor her traditional foreign suppliers can be readily resuscitated without a long-term investment programme which also assumes a constancy of demand. Given these definite restraints the Japanese Government is hopeful that by 1980 Japan's domestic coal production will have levelled off at a steady 20 million tons per year, with half as much again being imported.

Energy Demand Programme

Having examined a variety of measures to restrain energy demand, and having become accustomed to a new high-cost

energy situation, it is salutary to examine the forward planning
of Japan's likely energy demand. The almost incredible prediction is that despite all the efforts by both Government and
private industry to conserve energy, the whole trend of the
Japanese industrial juggernaut is towards increasing energy
consumption, so that by 1985 energy demand will have doubled
the 1973 figure. Breaking down such a prediction into its
components, it is expected that in 1985 Japan will consume
760 million kilolitres of energy of which 63 per cent will
comprise imported oil (cf. 73 per cent in 1973), 9.6 per cent
nuclear fuel (6 per cent in 1973) and 7.9 per cent natural gas.
Such predictions are based on an average real growth rate of 6.6
per cent over the decade 1975–85. Apart from the relentless
long-term upward trend in energy demand, with all that it
implies for the nature of Japanese society, to which the 1973
oil embargo and price rises provided only a temporary check,
the most surprising feature of the 1985 predictions was the
revelation that Japan is likely to remain heavily dependent on
imported energy.

Specifically the demand programme predicts that by 1985
something like 82 per cent of Japan's energy will be imported
and 8 per cent derived from domestic sources of supply. The
remaining 10 per cent, classified as a semi-domestic, is likely
to be provided from nuclear sources which, while they are
manufactured domestically, contain vital imported elements in
their composition. For a nation so poorly endowed with natural
energy resources Japan has devoted a comparatively meagre
proportion of her financial resources to developing her nuclear
energy potential for fairly obvious historical reasons. Nevertheless her nuclear energy industry has existed since the mid-1950s
and is capable of fairly rapid expansion if the political climate
should commend it. It is interesting that in 1975 the news that
4000 tons of nuclear waste was to be shipped from Japan to
Britain for storage created adverse attention in Britain. The
reason given for such an apparently bizarre trading transaction
is that Britain, having a more advanced nuclear energy industry
than Japan, has greater expertise and facilities for such bulk
nuclear waste storage. The suspicion remains that Japanese
public opinion is overwhelmingly more sensitive to the risks of
nuclear waste than are the British public.

Conclusion

As we saw at the beginning of this chapter, Japanese energy policy is important not only for its own sake but also because Japan is one of the superstates with wide external ramifications flowing from whatever foreign economic policies she chooses to pursue. It is also significant because of the high level of energy imports and the pattern adopted by a major industrial power which has no possibility of achieving energy self-sufficiency. At the same time, Japan's very lack of capacity to sustain herself from her own natural resources, most especially her lack of primary energy resources, has led her into a pattern of resource diplomacy likely to greatly enlarge her political sphere of influence, especially in Asia. While she would strenuously deny it as a conscious aim of her foreign policy, like both the Soviet Union and China, Japan is effectively creating a sphere of influence in Asia, not for any ideological or strategic motivation, but simply because she needs both the raw materials and the export markets to maintain her position as a major industrial power — the richest and most powerful in Asia.

After the disastrous conclusion to Japan's phase of imperialist expansion, the concept of an Asian co-prosperity sphere promoted during that fatal period is not one which Japan consciously wishes to pursue. Japan's leaders are all too aware of the veiled hostility which lingers on as a residue of that time when Japan stood momentarily as the greatest Asian power — an unspoken fear of a revived, economically expansionist Japan which might one day assert its strength — floating like a suspicious cloud all the way from Peking to Canberra. After thirty years of political eclipse, existing under virtual American tutelage, the very act of agreeing major concrete commercial joint projects with both the Communist superstates has brought Japan back into the sort of balanced set of relationships which an independent great power necessarily creates for itself.

Perhaps one of the best statements of the Japanese position in terms of the kind of role she feels disposed to play in the future concert of the nations, and especially in the energy field, was expressed in the Diet in early 1974 by the then Prime Minister, Kakuei Tanaka. He reminded his fellow parliamentarians that in the three decades since the end of the Second

World War Japan had risen from the ruins of that conflict by three stages, which he termed economic rehabilitation, the creation of a self-reliant economy, and cooperation within the international economy. Japan, he reflected, had become a principal industrial power in the world, despite its lack of either natural resources or capital, because of the applied intelligence and sustained efforts of its people. Like other industrial powers it had reached the point of becoming aware of numerous contradictions in the character of its prosperity, of which prices, pollution and energy were among the most pressing. In the field of prices, Tanaka, after referring to the major cause of the problem in the shape of cutbacks in the supply of oil and a multiple increase in its imported price, went on to list the Government's legislative remedies – the People's Life Stabil- isation Law, Petroleum Supply-and-Demand Adjustment Law, and the Law of Emergency Measures Against Cornering and Hoarding Goods.

The Government's positive overall remedy, he went on, was to stabilise the supply of natural resources as a whole, especially Japan's over-dependence on oil. This would be accomplished by speeding up the development of atomic energy and reviewing the role of both hydro-electric power and coal. Finance would also be set aside to promote the development of solar energy for the somewhat longer-term future. Meanwhile the Government would be making a two-pronged effort, internally to readjust the structure of the economy, externally both to diversify the sources of supply of raw materials and to ensure that such sources remained stable. As Tanaka noted, the securing of stable sources of food supply was among Japan's most urgent tasks, a task likely to become more difficult as the world population increased by leaps and bounds and weather conditions remained a threat to the reliability of the principal harvests. Unlike the case of energy there was considerable scope for developing the degree of Japanese self-sufficiency in agriculture. Accordingly the Japanese government would improve the productive base for agriculture, forestry and fishing, while especially encouraging the production of barley, soya beans and livestock. If Japan could find no way round the importing of the major proportion of her energy requirements for the foreseeable future she would most certainly strive towards self-sufficiency in food.

At first sight the Tanaka statement of Japan's broad economic objectives, since substantially restated by his successor, and the role that energy and natural resources are likely to play in the next five to ten years, is commendably balanced. While seeking to keep the Japanese industrial ship-of-state on course he acknowledges the greater priority that needs to be given to social and environmental factors. There must also be considerable admiration for the manner in which the Japanese Government and people responded to the very real threat presented to their way of life by the oil embargo and price rises. Nevertheless, while the response of Japan's leadership probably reflects the views of the majority of its citizens, there are disturbing signs that it seems to ignore the dissatisfaction of a large proportion of its younger citizens who are critical of the headlong pursuit of affluence and its seemingly insatiable demand for energy. Moreover, there are growing bands of extremist groups among the young whose dissatisfaction with society and the nature of Japanese industrialism in particular commands some sympathy, however much one may deplore the totally destructive means they have chosen to express that dissatisfaction.

To the question, why are such extremist groups proliferating, there is no single easy answer. According to their own propaganda their targets vary from Japanese imperialism, big business and the capitalist structure to Japanese economic expansion in south east Asia and a host of more particular offences against their political credo. Apart from their generally left-wing orientation they have it in common that they believe that their minority concerns have no opportunity of being expressed within the contemporary Japanese power structure. While at the moment they remain small if very active minorities, claiming of course, as is the wont of such groups, to represent the views and interests of a much larger proportion of the population (the accuracy of which claim it is virtually impossible to determine), there is a very real chance of their gaining increasing numbers of recruits. The question that must be faced sooner or later is, will the relentlessly upward long-term trend in Japanese energy consumption, with its attendant centralisation and bureaucratisation in both the public and private sectors, increasingly indistinguishable in their mode of operations, simply fuel the underlying dissatisfactions of a sufficiently large number of people that the extremists will gain ground even among the ideologically uncommitted?

The Japanese dilemma raises in an acute form a fundamental conflict which exists in greater or lesser degree in every one of the five superstates that we have examined in this short comparative survey: namely, the extent to which the acceptance of the continued high priority of increasing consumption in the Western superstates, and its apparent increasing adoption by the two Communist superstates, will mean such a growth in energy consumption that the liberty of the individual citizen will be irretrievably eroded. For the very character of the structures which arise to allocate resources efficiently in a high energy consumption industrial society are likely to lead to such a concentration of economic and political power that minorities of all kinds will become powerless to the extent that they can be safely disregarded. It is in such conditions that minorities, initially imbued with some just cause and at times more concerned and certainly more aware of the general interest than the increasingly isolated power elite, turn in utter frustration to extremism. Unable to discriminate between the just and the unjust causes of the extremists, the pressures pushing the power elites towards non-libertarian policies, if only to protect the legitimate rights of the majority whose interests are indiscriminately identified with the current structures, become irresistible.

The Japanese experience provides ample evidence that the very qualities that have enabled the Japanese economy to modify its structures to take account of the energy scarcity without fundamentally altering its economic priorities have also perpetuated a system which will inevitably alienate a growing proportion of the population, especially those who value individual freedom more highly than an unrestricted increase in material wealth. The dissent from the Left may seem the more vocal in Japan because the conspicuous waste, pollution and impersonality of big government and big business acting in concert engender a desire for a system at once more austere and idealistic; elsewhere, in the United States for instance, the dissent arises as much from the traditional Right as the Left, as the demands of greater and greater energy consumption create a new twentieth-century leviathan composed of combined governmental and corporation interests whose most notable examples take the form of the military—industrial complex. The recent

plight of New York City underlines the threat from a very
different quarter, the welfare—public services lobby, which,
while it does not operate directly on high energy consumption,
indirectly assumes the financial benefits which such high energy
consuming structures provide for it. As its parliamentary
representatives attempt to pacify those who have not benefited
from the fruits of industrial prosperity, or those who merely
find them bitter to the taste, the possibility that Japan will
generate similar problems to New York City is not as
improbable as it might have been only a decade ago. The
political conservatism which has characterised the last thirty
years in Japan is fast becoming transformed, as the welfarism of
the major companies is being supplemented by a government
acknowledgement of responsibility for the social environment
which it has yet to reconcile with people's simultaneous
expectations of never-ending economic growth.

It is the scope of these modern leviathans which we have just
outlined: the possibilities for containing and redirecting them
by switching the pattern of energy production and consumption
and the education of the public on the necessity to choose
between spiralling energy consumption and its material benefits
or greater political freedom and social amenity. These are
among the central issues with which we will have to cope in the
remaining decades of the twentieth century. And beyond any
reform of the institutional structures of the superstates, however urgently reform may suggest itself, there is the question of
the values held by the individual citizens of each of the superstates. In the last analysis it is upon these individual values that
the prospect for institutional reform rests — whether, for
instance, a premium is to be set on the maintenance of current
patterns of accelerating energy consumption regardless of the
corrosive effects on personal liberty; such issues cannot finally
be determined except by the individual. To make available to
the individual an outline of the nature of the changes taking
place has been the chief object of this book.

Postscript: Dialogue or Confrontation?

In his 1975 Fawley Foundation lecture at Southampton University Lord Ashby, the eminent biologist and former chairman of Britain's Royal Commission on Environmental Pollution, commenting on the predicted exhaustion of non-renewable resources, said that

> the imminent danger is not the collapse of affluent societies due to material famine or excesses. It is collapse due to political and social disintegration. And the urgent task is not to protect our great-great-grandchildren: it is to do something about human communities already suffering from these threatened ultimate perils.
>
> If our political systems do not respond to these known, present and well publicized disasters they are hardly likely to respond to the possibility, however plausible, that similiar disasters might occur after we have been in our graves for a century or more.

While these remarks were primarily addressed to the more affluent societies where economic growth has outstripped regulation of the growth process, their relevance to the world economy as a whole cannot be underestimated. For if one principle has been commonly embraced since the 1973 Middle East war it is the inescapable interdependence of the developed and developing countries in the last quarter of the twentieth century. The importance of any attempts to create a lasting and mutually advantageous structure embracing the industrialised and non-industrialised nations can readily be appreciated.

The Paris meeting in December 1975 to discuss the energy and raw material issue only two years after a dramatic fourfold increase in the price of oil that shook the industrialised and non-industrialised world alike, represented at the very least a response to a vitally important range of problems. The

144

expectations of the two main sides — those of the developing countries and oil producers to draw up the outlines of what has been described as a New Economic Order which would somehow shift the balance of wealth toward the non--industrialised countries, and the industrial countries who need to maintain security of supply for raw materials for themselves while creating a framework for greater prosperity for the non-industrial states — are not to be realised with the dramatic suddenness of the oil producers. Yet it was the example of the OPEC states, built upon the cumulative failure of successive attempts to achieve greater parity between the industrial and non-industrial countries during the last decade in particular, that has raised the expectations of the non-industrial countries that reserves of primary commodities can be used to achieve political parity and economic prosperity. Putting aside the immediate achievements of the Paris conference in creating four commissions on energy, finance, raw materials and development as being a worthwhile preliminary step toward some form of dialogue, one must raise the fundamental question of whether the expectations held by many of the developing countries and not a few Western commentators are realistically based?

It is true that the developed countries, taken together, are heavily dependent on imports of raw materials from the developing countries (as they are increasingly on the Communist countries); but it is also true that the Western industrial countries are the largest exporters of primary products.[1] More precisely, 50 per cent of world exports of primary commodities originate in Western industrial countries compared with 40 per cent from the non-industrial countries and the remaining 10 per cent from Communist countries. Moreover, while the developing countries absorb only about one-sixth of all world primary exports (compared with three-quarters absorbed by the developed countries), that one-sixth represents around one-quarter of their total imports. Indeed, for the non oil-exporting developing countries imports of primary commodities account for one third of their total imports. Most surprisingly to the casual observer, two-thirds of primary product imports into the developing countries are comprised of essential foodstuffs, chiefly imported from industrial countries. If the foregoing percentages illustrate the degree of inter-dependence between the industrial and non-industrial countries they also raise fundamental questions over the effectiveness and even the advisability of creating producer cartels in the manner of the OPEC oil cartel. Though it has proved successful for the handful of oil-exporting countries, largely thanks to the resolution of Saudi Arabia and Kuwait, even the OPEC cartel can reasonably be expected to loosen its grip over time as alternative energy sources are developed. The reasons why attempts at international cartels over the last one hundred years have generally failed are more numerous than we can elaborate here. They include such stringent preconditions as the neccessity for the cartel to control around two-thirds of the total market supply, including a very substantial proportion of the reserves which are commercially exploitable. The dangers of the failure of attempts to create commodity cartels fall just as heavily on the producers as on the consumers, since the former normally require a steady flow of foreign exchange earnings and, not least, sustained investment as surely as the consumer countries require stable sources of supply. And while it is probable that the greater part of the as yet undiscovered reserves of most of the world's major raw materials lie underground in the developing countries the prospect is that they will forever remain there unless sufficient technical capacity and investment is channelled to it from the Western industrial countries. Even before the oil price rises the developing countries suffered from a scarcity of development capital; now that shortage has become much more acute.

Thus for the general reasons just surveyed it is in the interests of both industrial and non-industrial countries to de-escalate the confrontation which since 1973 has been gathering momentum. If the issues are divested of their ideological content it will be apparent that the requirement of the industrial countries for a steady flow of commodities at reasonable price levels is in no way incompatible with the non-industrial countries' desire to accelerate their economic and social development. Such progress can only be achieved, however, within a mutually agreed set of rules and an atmosphere of toleration and compromise. Apart from the simple fact that excepting tin, phosphates and bauxite there is no major mineral besides oil that lends itself to a producer commodity cartel, it would be counter productive to the interests of the non-industrial countries as a whole, just as

the OPEC cartel has hurt the economies of the very poorest
non-industrial countries more than any single industrial
country. This can be realised when it is remembered that
relatively few developing countries export substantial quantities
of minerals. Thus at the end of the 1960s it was estimated that
90 per cent of all mineral exports from non-industrial countries
derived from countries containing a mere 25 per cent of the
Third World's total population. The oil-producing states,
expecially the Arab oil-exporting nations, illustrate this concentration of mineral wealth in relatively sparsely populated
countries. Furthermore, if mineral prices were raised too high
too fast in the world market it would preclude the commercial
development of manufacturing industries, especially the
processing of domestic raw materials for the domestic market as
well as for export.

To conclude on what one hopes is a note of optimistic
realism: as long as the mutual interests of the industrial and
non-industrial countries are taken into full account and an
honest attempt is made to resolve the differences on a
pragmatic series of mutual trade-offs, the dialogue between the
world's north and south axis will yield long-term dividends.
However, should the advocates of forced changes win the day
under the misplaced conviction that the historical differences in
the economic development of the industrial and non-industrial
countries can most effectively be bridged by means of political
confrontation, every nation will be the loser. But the poorest
and the weakest will be the chief victims of a politically induced
confrontation since the system is bound to reflect the economic
imbalance which has existed for a very considerable time and
which can only be bridged by sustained policies of internal
development in the poor countries themselves. A new international economic framework is in itself insufficient; there must
also be a favourable political climate for development. Such
conditions, if they are to be created at all, are most likely to
arise from realistic and sustained negotiations within the Tokyo
Round of the General Agreement on Tariffs and Trade (GATT).
Nobody should be complacent about the great gulf of in-
equality which divides the industrialised and non-industrialised
nations along a north—south axis. But if that gulf is to be
bridged it will not be done by wielding the supposed political

weapon of raw materials — coercion is as longstanding an enemy
of durable economic and social progress as total unconcern —
but by the painstaking creation of the means of partnership
between the better and less well-off nations who manifestly
need each other as never before in history.

References

1 The United States
1. Richard M. Nixon, *U.S. foreign policy for the 1970s: shaping a durable peace.* A report to the Congress (3 May 1973).
2. Christopher Thorne, *The Limits of Foreign Policy.* Hamish Hamilton, London; George Putnam, New York (1972).
3. W. W. Rostow, *The Diffusion of Power.* Macmillan, New York (1972).
4. *The U.S. Congressional Bulletin.*
5. Hearings before the Subcommittee on International Trade, the Committee of Finance, the U.S. Senate Ninety-Third Congress (February, March 1973).
6. Wayne Wilcox, United States: imperial recession. *International Affairs* (October 1973).

2 The European Economic Community

1. Meeting Europe's Energy Requirements, National Coal Board (UK), 1962.
2. First Guidelines for a Community Energy Policy (EEC Commission, December, 1968).
3. Bulletin of the European Communities, Supplement 4/74, Towards a new energy policy strategy for the European community.
4. Promoting the utilization of nuclear energy, Bull. EC2 1974.
5. The Community's relations with the energy producing countries, Bull. EC1 1974.

3 The Soviet Union

1. Robert W. Campbell, *The Economics of Soviet Oil and Gas.* Johns Hopkins University Press, Baltimore (1968).
2. Robert N. North, Soviet northern development: the case of north-western Siberia. *Soviet Studies* (October 1972).
3. M. A. Adelman, *The World Petroleum Market.* Johns Hopkins University Press, Baltimore (1972).
4. Robert W. Campbell, Some issues in the Soviet energy policy of the seventies. In *Soviet Economic Policy for the 1970s, a compendium for the U.S. Congress* (1973).
5. J. Richard Lee, The Soviet petroleum industry: promise and problems. In *Soviet Economic Policy for the 1970s: a compendium for the U.S. Congress* (1973).
6. Iain F. Elliot, *The Soviet Energy Balance.* Praeger, New York and London.

4   China

1. Wang Gungwu, Chinese society and foreign policy. *International Affairs* (October 1972).
2. Robert Carin, Power industry in Communist China. Hong Kong University (1963).
3. Yuan-Li Wu, *Economic Development and the Use of Energy Resources in Communist China*. Praeger, New York and London.
4. Sino-British Trade Council, *China's Oil Industry*.
5. Tatsu Kambara, The petroleum industry in China. *China Quarterly* (December 1974).
6. *Peking Review*, issues extending from October 1973 to October 1975.

5   Japan

1. A. M. Halpern, Japan: economic giant's quiet diplomacy. *International Affairs* (October 1973).
2. Kiyoshi Kojima, *Japanese Foreign Economic Policy*. Trade Policy Research Centre, London.
3. Hugh Corbet *et al.*, *Trade Strategy and the Asian—Pacific Region*. Allen and Unwin, London, University of Toronto, Toronto.
4. Industrial Review of Japan, 1975. *Japan Economic Journal*, Tokyo (1975).
5. Toshiyuki Shirai, Government economic policy highlights. *Japan Economic Review*, Tokyo (January 1975).
6. Haruki Niwa, Prospects for another economic miracle in Japan. *Japan Echo*, Tokyo, II, no. 2 (1975).

Postscript
1. An excellent analysis of the principal issues in the current debate on a new framework for world commodity trade is to be found in Hugh Corbet's *Raw Materials*, published by the Trade Policy Research Centre (1975), to which the author is indebted for some of the vital figures in this Postscript.

Index

S. KATHARINE'S COLLEGE
LIBRARY

121063